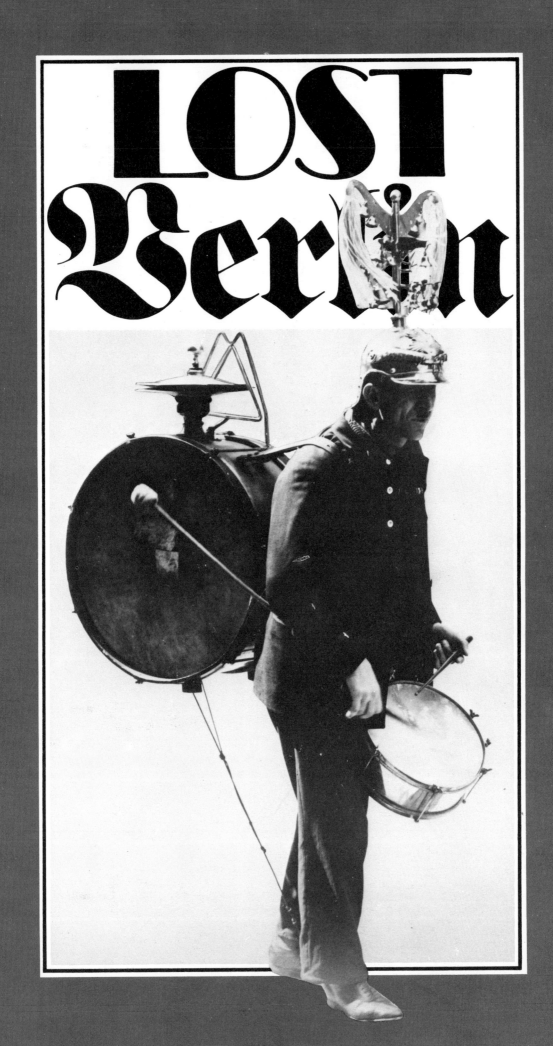

LOST
Berlin

SUSANNE EVERETT

ST. MARTIN'S PRESS
NEW YORK

A BISON BOOK

Published in the USA in 1981 by

St. Martin's Press Inc.
175 Fifth Avenue,
New York, NY 10016
USA

Copyright © 1979 Bison Books Limited

First Published in the UK in 1979 by

Bison Books Limited
4 Cromwell Place
London SW7

Library of Congress Catalog Card Number 80-54584
ISBN 0-312-49879-9

Susanne Everett

Printed in Hong Kong

LOST Berlin

CONTENTS

BERLINERLUFT

An 1889 Locarno automobile passes through the
Brandenburg Gate in 1925 traffic.

The inhabitants of the city of Berlin—or rather those most elusive of characters, the Berliners—have a motto: 'Berlin bleibt noch Berlin.' ('Berlin is still Berlin'). Berlin is, indeed, still Berlin. It is still a city of trees and birds, music and drama, tension and excitement. It still has its canals, lakes and rivers, its special light and its exhilarating air. But it is not one city but two, and the grim barbed-wire barrier between them serves as a perpetual reminder, not only of the division between east and west, but of a world now vanished forever. For beneath the reconstructed city lies buried the heart of Imperial Berlin, that ugly, grandiose realization of Bismarck's dream of empire, together with the remains of Weimar and the monstrous skeleton of the Third Reich.

Between 1943 and 1945 allied bombers destroyed a third of the city's 1.5 million buildings, laying waste to ten square miles of central Berlin and killing or injuring 150,000 people. In 1945 after the bombing had stopped, the Russians turned 22,000 guns on what was left and razed it to the ground. Gone were the public monuments, the elaborate façades, the libraries and the university. The Unter den Linden, that wide and stately boulevard lined with linden trees, was reduced to an unrecognizable pile of rubble. The State Opera House was gutted, the Imperial Palace damaged beyond repair. The beerhalls and cafes on the Kurfürstendamm lay in ruins. The Romanische Cafe on the Tauentzienstrasse, the Adlon Hotel at No 1 Unter den Linden, the Kaiserhof Hotel, Hitler's headquarters before he came to power, and the Chancellery, in which so many infamous Nazi plots were hatched, all suffered the same fate. Even the supposedly impregnable Tiergarten flaktower, into which the priceless contents of the Kaiser Wilhelm Museum were transferred during the war, crumbled to dust, its heavy concrete slabs crushing indiscriminately Rembrandts, Titians, and Rubens together with the best of Heinrich Schliemann's Trojan excavations, among them the golden mask of Priam. The animals, too, perished in large numbers—those that did not die in the flames during the air raids either starved to death or were caught up in crossfire when the Tiergarten became a battlefield during the last weeks of the war. Of the original 4000, only 91 survived.

The zoo has been restocked and, for East Berliners, a 400-acre Tierpark created in Friedrichsfelde, described by

Berlin. Brandenburger Tor

one writer as 'a flower-filled wildlife preserve with streams filled with exotic fish, the banks of these streams crowded with rare water birds and a span of trees and bushes filled with other birds of all kinds . . .' which, he added, provided them 'not only with its natural delights, but also with a respite from propaganda.' On both sides of the wall a new city has risen from the ashes of the old—administrative buildings, recreation facilities, shops, restaurants, banks, concert halls, theaters and modern housing developments. Trees have been planted along the streets and churches rebuilt or restored. 'The whole city,' wrote *The Sunday Times* journalist, Michael Ratcliffe, 'is one great image, or rather a collection of contradictory images. . . . The mind requires a kind of double vision, assimilating both the ambiguous present and the gaunt, nudging past. Surely no city in the world—not Rome, not Pompeii—suffuses such an appalling sense of history. . . .'

Some of the physical reminders of the past are more visible than others. The huge Reichstag still stands to the north of the Brandenburg Gate, but stripped of all its legislative powers it has become just another office building. Visitors to the new Jewish Community Center, built in 1958, can see in the old doorway and pillar incorporated into its façade an allusion to the Central Synagogue burned down by the Nazis during the *Kristallnacht* of twenty years

Right: The monument of Frederick the Great, the man who led Prussia to greatness in the 1880s.
Below: The Brandenburg Gate was built by Carl Langhaus in 1789 to celebrate Prussia's victories.

Above: The German National Gallery in Berlin, whose great collection was destroyed by the Nazis and the war.
Left: Berlin's Dom (cathedral) was built on the central island in the Spree in the early 1900s.
Right: The Dom is linked to the mainland by the Kurfürsten Bridge.

before. The tower of the ugly Kaiser Wilhelm Memorial Church, on the other hand, the only part of the building left standing and itself gutted by fire during an air raid, was only preserved after heated discussion—many Berliners claiming, with some justice, that it was not a 'symbol of democratic Berlin.' Its supporters managed to save it, on the equally justifiable pretext that it was 'an eternal reminder of the destruction caused by war,' and it now stands flanked by a new, octagonal church on one side and a new tower on the other. The Communists rebuilt the Opera House, but demolished what was left of the Imperial Palace, renaming the vacant space Marx-Engels Platz. They did, however, preserve the balcony from which Karl Liebknecht proclaimed the German Revolution in 1918. This relic of revolutionary fervor is now, as Otto Friedrich remarked, 'literally embedded' in the State Council building on the south side of the square—presumably in the hope that it will provide an inspiration to any recalcitrant Berliner intent on evading the ideological pressures imposed on him by his doggedly reformist masters.

The severe doctrines preached by their Russian mentors have not yet completely managed to eradicate the East Berliners' insatiable appetite for the pleasures of eating, drinking and dancing in public places. Although deprived of many of their old haunts, they have created new nightspots. Instead of the Cafe Bauer they have the Linden Corso, where the 'concert cafe,' the wine restaurant, the upstairs dance bar and the tables outside on the pavement create the illusion that nothing has changed. Next door in the *Nachtbar* (Nightbar) those who can afford it (mainly East Berlin functionaries) 'sip Russian vodka, Slavic wines, and the products of the GDR's own "People-owned" distillery.' Less well-heeled East Berliners have to make do with snack bars, most of which offer a monotonous diet of sausage and beer (except for the one opposite the Soviet Military Cemetery in Treptow, which apparently attempts to divert its customers by offering them the added attraction of watching slides of Red Army graves while they eat).

And in the west, to cater for the ever-increasing flood of curious tourists, bright modern hotels have been built to replace those early twentieth-century temples of the great, the Adlon, the Kaiserhof and the Fürstenhof, and those haunts of the louche and rich, the Eden and the Bristol. The Hilton, the Bristol-Hotel-Kempinski, the Hotel Berlin, serve their purpose well, but the splendor and the glamor have gone. When William Shirer, the distinguished Berlin representative of the Columbia Broadcasting Company, returned to the city after the war, he went to look for the Adlon, where he had lived for a time. He found nothing but a shell, but 'there was a sign' (he wrote in his diary) 'on the battered front door . . . through which I had passed so often in my Berlin years. It announced bravely that "Five o'clock Tea" was being served.

"But where?" I asked . . . (for) through the broken walls of the once famous hostelry you could see nothing but debris.

"In the cellar" was the reply. "And some of the old waiters are still around in their long, formal coats and starched collars just as if nothing has changed." '

In their attempt to preserve some semblance of order in their shattered world the staff at the Adlon provided some evidence for Heinrich Heine's idealistic theory that Berlin was 'not really a city at all' but only a 'locality where a group of people, and among them people of fine minds, congregate,' people who, he added, 'are quite indifferent to the locality,' but who 'constitute the spiritual Berlin.' Heine, however, was writing in the eighteenth century, and, although Berlin had been transformed into a royal capital by Frederick I, Great-Elector of Brandenburg-Prussia (the first ruler to succumb openly to the Prussian obsession with Great Power status by obtaining for himself the title of 'King' in Prussia), and although it was given a veneer of cultural acceptability by his grandson, the 'philosopher king,' Frederick the Great, it remained a provincial town. It had not yet enjoyed the strange and brilliant fusion of a hitherto fragmented culture, that extraordinary and peculiarly German renaissance which turned Berlin for a brief fourteen years during the troubled period of the Weimar Republic into what has been called 'the most exciting city in the world,' attracting (before it was snuffed out by censorship, oppression and persecution) like moths around a

Far left: The Potsdamerstrasse leading to the Potsdamerplatz in 1930. This was the main road to Potsdam, the home of the Hohenzollern monarchs.
Left: The Unter den Linden at the corner of the Friedrichstrasse. The Unter den Linden was designed and built by Knobelsdorff at Frederick the Great's instigation.
Below: The Friedrichstrasse at the corner of the Leipzigerstrasse.
Below right: View from the Schön (beautiful) Café on the Unter den Linden. This famous avenue was destroyed during the war and is now in East Berlin.

candleflame the most talented, the most flamboyant and the most decadent elements in Europe.

'Social and political factors,' said W H Bruford in his book, *Germany in the Eighteenth Century*, 'exercise at all times a pervasive influence on culture in general, an influence which is nonetheless important for being difficult to trace with any final certainty.' Professor Bruford explained how political, economic and social factors affected the German literary revival in the eighteenth century, and also untangled the intricacies of German provincial history before 1871. (After 1871 Bismarck made everything easier by welding the numerous small states together into a unified whole, giving them one German Emperor, one German government and one German capital city.)

His words are, however, equally applicable to Germany of the 1920s. Fortified by hindsight, various historians have attempted to account for the combination of the rational and the frenetic which injected a vigorous cultural life into Berlin at a time when the country was demoralized by defeat in war, drained of resources, crippled by inflation and prey to warring revolutionary factions. In a rash of nostalgic fervor claims have been made that are as inaccurate as they are hard to substantiate. Berlin has been called a 'doomed' city and its 'flowering' compared with Rome toward the end of the Republic.

But Weimar was by no means 'doomed'—many felt the Republic could survive—and to see the literary and artistic world of Berlin in the Twenties as a culmination of, rather than a stage in the development of, Germany's cultural life is to deny it its place in German history. It is to forget the importance of the German renaissance during the early sixteenth century; it is to forget the influence of Luther, who had an effect so deep that, in the view of A J P Taylor, 'Germany is the Germany of Luther to this day. . . . In Luther was implicit the emotionalism of the Romantic movement, the German nationalist sense of being different, above all the elevation of feeling over thinking which is characteristic of modern Germany'; it is to forget the classic and romantic movements in literature and music, the development of German philosophical thought and the

growth and standing of the universities; it is to forget the origins of the printing industry, the cultural cosmopolitanism of Goethe, Schiller, Wieland and Kant, and the music of Bach, Beethoven, Brahms and Wagner; and it is to deny Weimar, Hamburg, Mannheim, Leipzig, Dresden, Nuremberg, Munich and Bayreuth their rightful place in the hierarchy of German intellectual tradition.

None of these towns or cities were, however, more than principal centers of *Kleinstaaterai*, or 'little states,' and they remained, in the absence of a major capital city, satellites without a sun, drawing their intellectual sustenance from Paris or Vienna. Germany had nowhere, as Goethe complained, where 'the best minds of a great nation are assembled in one place, teaching and stimulating each other in daily intercourse, contention and rivalry, where the best products of nature and art from every corner of the earth are always there for them to see with their own eyes, where they are reminded whenever they cross a bridge or a square of a great past and where every street corner has seen history in the making.'

Until 1871 Berlin remained just such another provincial center and, for all its 'royal' status was merely the sandy, remote capital of Prussia, itself only one of at least 300 sovereign states, each with their princelings and each jockeying for power and influence within the Holy Roman Empire. By the end of the eighteenth century, however, largely due to Frederick II (Frederick the Great), whose craving for territory and obsession with militarism led him into 'an almost unbroken succession of wars,' Prussia was the dominant power in Germany north of the Main river. And after the battle of Leipzig in 1814 which ended the humiliating occupation of Berlin by the French after Napoleon defeated the Prussian army in 1806, she claimed and was awarded at the Congress of Vienna further extensions to her territory, namely Rhineland from Coblenz to Cologne and much of Saxony. Austria, however, dashed Prussian hopes of becoming president of the replacement for the Holy Roman Empire, the newly-formed *Deutsche Bund* (a confederation of 39 states sending delegates to an assembly at Frankfurt-am-Main) by assuming the role herself.

The birth of German liberalism—an ideal with which the German middle class toyed in the years between 1815 and 1848 and which came to a head during the revolutions of 1848, stemmed largely from the resentment caused by this ascendant maneuver of Austria's, coming as it did at a moment when Prussia was weakened and demoralized by the events of 1806–15. The liberals saw the Prussian obsession with ascendancy within the Bund as a threat to German unity and dedicated themselves both to reforming and centralizing the cumbersome German political system and to reducing the power of the Prussian and the Austrian armies.

Below: A view of the south side of the Unter den Linden, numbers 28–32.

In March 1848 there were violent outbreaks of rioting in Vienna and Berlin. In Berlin the demonstrators appeared to have triumphed—the easily-swayed and mentally unstable Frederick IV called off his Prussian troops rather than see them 'subdue his own people by force,' eventually ordering them to withdraw unconditionally. He then drove through the streets wearing the revolutionary colors of national Germany, and openly pledged himself to the nationalist cause, promising that 'Henceforth Prussia will merge with Germany.'

As a result of Frederick's temporary co-operation, the apparent capitulation of the Prussian army and the subsequent acquiescence of the rest of the German princes, the liberals were able to embark on their self-imposed task of 'uniting Germany by consent.' Although, however, there were constitutional reforms—a new national assembly was elected on universal or existing suffrage and the Prussian parliament was reconvened on a democratic basis—the delegates, many of whom were academics and none of whom had any experience of politics at a national level, found the complexities of drawing up a constitution which combined social order with reconciliation within the Bund

Left: The famous Adlon Hotel on the Unter den Linden. During the 1920s it was a meeting place for politicians, journalists and writers.
Below: The goldfish pond in the Tiergarten, the central park in Berlin.

more taxing than they had first thought. To add to their problems, the 'east Germans' in Bohemia and Poland displayed inconveniently nationalistic minds of their own. To bring them to their senses and to uphold the cause of German nationalism, the liberals supported the armed intervention of Prussia and Austria, with the result that, under their very noses, the two military monarchies were able to regain their former positions of political power based on armed strength, which they had enjoyed until 1848. By the end of the year Berlin was under martial law and by January 1849 Prussia was once more a constitutional monarchy 'with the accent on Monarch.'

The death of German liberalism and the failure of the Berlin revolution were largely due to the impractical nature of the revolutionaries themselves. The 'masses,' whom they hoped to benefit by their radical behavior, were in the first place not mobilized and in the second not considered. A further, and ultimately fatal, weakness was the inability of liberals to recognize the true power of Prussian militarism, many believing that Prussia's dominant urges could be curbed if only the constitution were reformed.

When German unification did eventually occur just over twenty years later, it was as a result of war, not reasonable debate, and its creation was due to one Prussian autocrat, Count Otto von Bismarck-Schönhausen. The defeat of Austria by Prussia at the battle of Königgratz (Sadowa) in Bohemia on 3 July 1866, settled once and for all the perennial problem of the German leadership and established the dominance of Prussia in Germany. During the Seven Weeks' War some German states, notably Bavaria, Württemberg, Saxony and Hanover, sided with Austria

against Prussia, but with Austria's defeat became subject to Prussian rule. Four years later, therefore, Bismarck having maneuvered France into a war with Prussia, the French were faced by a united Germany for the first time. Subsequent German victories over the French army, then said to be the best in Europe, were a dramatic show of Prussian military strength and paved the way for the realization of Bismarck's imperial ambitions—ambitions which were finally achieved after the surrender of Napoleon III at Sedan on 1 September 1870.

The Empire was officially proclaimed on 18 January 1871 in the Gallery of Mirrors at the Royal Palace of Versailles (an ostentatious and tasteless gesture the French were not to forget and for which, forty years later, the Germans paid a heavy price). The new constitution, drawn up by Bismarck with himself as Chancellor, cleverly concealed the fact that although there were two elected houses, the Bundesrat (upper house) and the Reichstag (lower house), and although the power of the imperial government had been limited to the 'bare essentials in order to avoid any infringement on the susceptibilities of individual states,' all real power was conserved in the hands of the Emperor, his Chancellor and his Ministers.

The titular head of the Empire became the aging Wilhelm I, and its capital and center of government Berlin. In 1871 Berlin was still a provincial city, albeit an elegant one, its center dominated by the Royal Palace and the *Forum Fredericianum* (a large square containing a theater, more palaces and some public buildings) and flanked by various small villages, Schöneberg, Friedenau, Wilmersdorf, Charlottenburg and Westend. The benefits of Empire,

Left: The Markgrafen at the corner of Junkerstrasse.
Below: Policemen on horseback prepare for demonstrations outside the Reichstag in 1930.

Below: The Reichstag was a heavy tribute to Renaissance architecture, which was opened in 1894. It is still standing after some renovation.

Left: The Fischerstrasse in Berlin's Old City.
Right: The illuminated front of the Hermann Tietz department store at the Hallesches Gate.
Far right: The Mühldamm Lock over the Spree, after its renovation.

however, soon began to make themselves felt. Vast reparations were extracted from the French—another source of humiliation for which the French wreaked their revenge in 1918—and five billion francs were injected into the economy 'stimulating it to fever pitch.'

Berlin became a boom city; investors fell over themselves to put their money in 'real estate, railways, construction firms, banks and insurance companies.' The first issue of the *Berliner Tageblatt*, launched in 1871 by Rudolf Messe, announced: 'At a time when the eyes of the world look toward Berlin, we present to the public the *Berliner Tageblatt*. The capital of Prussia has become the capital of Germany, a metropolis, a world city. . . . We must be inspired by the thought that he who writes for Berlin, writes for the civilized world.'

It took over twenty years, however, for the metamorphosis from *grossstadt* (great city) to *weltstadt* (world city) to be completed. In 1865 the city contained 658,000 inhabitants, in 1875, 964,000 but by 1910 it had swelled to over two million. But late in 1892 the Kaiser Wilhelm II wrote from Norway: '. . . There is nothing in Berlin that can captivate the foreigner except a few museums, castles and soldiers. After six days, the red book in hand, he has seen everything and he departs relieved, feeling that he has done his duty,' adding, somewhat unfairly: 'The Berliner does not see these things, and would be very upset were he told about them.'

The Kaiser, however, had only himself to blame if he found Berlin dull and uninspiring, for it was due to his passion for the massive and grandiose that it became studded with buildings and monuments of gigantic ugliness. He was particularly fond of sculpture, considering it 'a symbolic expression of imperial might' and imperial Berlin soon began to bear witness to these sentiments. The sculptor Reinhold Begas was commissioned to design a monument to Wilhelm I (William the Victorious). It was erected in 1897 and *The Times* reported the statue as being '65.5 feet high, mounted on a bronze pedestal, resting on a cruciform block of granite, on each side of which lies a couchant lion in bronze. At the front and back of the pedestal are bronze shields bearing the inscriptions respectively, "Wilhelm the Great, German Emperor, King of Prussia, 1861-1888" and "In gratitude and true affection—the German people." At each corner stands a winged figure of Victory. On the sides are two allegorical scenes in relief representing war and peace.' The Berliners understood this monstrosity only too well—they nicknamed it 'William in the Lions' Den,' adding caustically 'That's the amount of bronze you can buy for four million marks.'

Left: The Friedrichstrasse railway station, which was situated at the northern end of the street.
Right: The Hotel Excelsior in Kreuzberg in 1930. Although not as famous as the Adlon, it ranked with the Bristol, Eden and Kaiserhof.

In the huge Königsplatz the triumphant conquest of France was commemorated by a vast column of victory, and on either side of the Siegesallee, the Kaiser's gift to the city, 32 enormous white marble monuments (also designed by the sycophantic Begas) testified to the glorious achievement of his Hohenzollern forebears. (A gift horse Berliners were prepared to look firmly in the mouth—they called it the 'avenue of the puppets' and the artist Max Liebermann complained that he 'needed dark glasses to look at this crime against good taste.')

Although Wilhelm II did not go quite as far as Hermann Göring, who is supposed to have said: 'When I hear the word "culture" I reach for my revolver,' neither he nor the Empress Augusta Victoria had much time for innovative art, preferring solidly representational subjects designed to flatter their self-esteem. As the Kaiser himself put it, at the inauguration of the Siegesalle in 1901: 'An art which transgresses the laws and barriers outlined by Me, ceases to be an art; it is merely a factory product, a trade, and art must never become such a thing. The often misused word "liberty" . . . leads to . . . license and presumption. . . . To us, the German people, ideals have become permanent possessions, whereas among other peoples they have been more or less lost. Only the German nation is left, and we are called upon to preserve, cultivate, and continue these great

Left: Berlin's busiest corner, the Unter den Linden and the Friedrichstrasse, seen from the Kranzler Café.
Below: The Kaiser Wilhelm Memorial Church seen from the Wittenbergplatz down the Tauentzienstrasse.
Right: Pedestrians in the Potsdamerplatz in 1930.

Above left: The Kaiser Wilhelm Memorial Church.
Below left: Flowers ladies in the Potsdamerplatz.
Above: A 'stilted' view of Berlin street theater.
Above right: Otto Witte, ex-King of Albania, told the story
of his three-day reign to Berliners in 1924.

ideals, and among those ideals is the duty to offer to the
toiling classes the possibility of elevating themselves to the
beautiful and of raising themselves above their ordinary
thoughts. If art, as so frequently happens now, does nothing
more than paint misery more ugly than it is, it sins against
the German people.'

Great ideals for the Kaiser were limited to public ex-
pressions of faith in himself as the head of an empire both
gloriously secure and magnificently optimistic. It was not
surprising, therefore, that the painter Adolf Menzel was a
great favorite, for his fascination with Prussian history and
his pictorial realism struck a chord with both Emperor and
Empress—they particularly admired Menzel's acknowledged masterpiece, a portrait of Wilhelm I in his carriage,
riding through the Unter den Linden before leaving for the
front in 1870.

Contemporary art, on the other hand, alarmed them. In
1909 the director of the Berlin National Gallery, Hugo
Tschudi, resigned after the Kaiser vetoed his decision to
buy the work of some French Impressionists. However,
despite the Kaiser's disapproval, the gallery eventually
acquired pictures by Monet, Manet, Renoir, Sisley and
Cézanne, but hung them out of his sight in 'a badly lit room
on the top floor.' And as for the 'secessionist' group of
painters led in Berlin by Max Liebermann and Walter

Leistikow, who exhibited their work in a gallery on the
Kurfürstendamm, they were completely beyond the pale—
the Kaiser became apopleptic, fulminating that it was 'art
from the gutter.' Even to look at such debased pictures was
tantamount to treason: 'Officers who wished to visit the
exhibition,' wrote one historian, 'were advised to wear
mufti.'

The Empress had a weakness for churches—the church
near the imperial castle, the official place of worship for the
Hohenzollerns, was replaced by a copy of St Peter's in
Rome, another sop to Hohenzollern *folies de grandeur* and
designed to 'show the grandiose development of Brandenburg-Prussia since the assumption of Hohenzollern leadership' (as was the building of the Kaiser Wilhelm Memorial
Church, erected at the entrance to the Kurfürstendamm).

The Kaiserin's piety also demanded a certain standard
of morality in the theater and the opera house. Richard
Strauss's opera *Salome*, first performed in Dresden in 1911,
was only allowed to be staged in Berlin after the management gave an assurance that 'a Star of Bethlehem would
rise at the end of the work.' Imperial sensibilities having
been appeased, the opera enjoyed considerable success—
it was performed fifty times in a single season. *Der Rosenkavalier* also suffered bowdlerization, this time at the hands
of the Kaiser, who objected to the 'uninhibited lustiness of
Baron Ochs von Lerchenau,' complaining that 'an imperial chamberlain should not act like a vulgar fellow.'
Strauss agreed to the proposed adjustments—he had, after
all, some interest in seeing his own work produced in
Berlin, having been appointed musical director of the
Hofoper in 1908.

Philistine and oppressive though the atmosphere was, Imperial Germany was not a dictatorship, and despite the Kaiser's conventional tastes many avant-garde movements managed to flourish in Berlin before 1914. German Expressionism, that 'violent, explicit manifestation of modernism,' which owed so much to the Norwegian Edvard Munch and the Russian Wassily Kandinsky, drew its inspiration from Nietzsche and the German Romantic movement. Its disciples believed in 'instinct, intuition and in a religious participation in the hidden processes of life' and were united in their opposition to classical or representational form, and in their desire to 'cultivate their inner life, articulate their religious yearning, and satisfy their dim longing for human and cultural renewal.' As early as 1901 Heinrich Mann published *Im Schlaraffenland* (Berlin, the Land of Cockaigne), a shrewd and savage portrait of contemporary Berlin society. In the same year his younger brother Thomas published the novel that brought him phenomenal success at the age of 26—*Buddenbrooks*. Wassily Kandinsky's revolutionary manifesto, *Uber das geistige in der Kunst*, appeared in 1912. Also by this time the two rival literary magazines, *Die Aktion* and *Der Sturm* were pursuing their policies of publishing the young, avant-garde literary generation.

Die Aktion, founded by Frank Pfemfert in 1911, was a mixture of articles on social problems, interpretations of Bakunin Kropotkin or Proudhon, and work by poets such as Gottfried Benn, Ernst Blass, Oskar Kanehl and Jacob von Hoddis. Von Hoddis wrote what has been described as the 'first nominally expressionist poem,' which appeared in the periodical in 1911. It was called *World's End* and was considered to be 'expressionist' according to Martin Seymour-Smith, because, 'as well as satirizing bourgeois complacency and ironically predicting disaster, it presented what Michael Hamburger has called "an arbitrary concatenation of images derived from contemporary life . . . a picture but not a realistic one."' Herwarth Walden, editor of *Der Sturm*, not only published articles, poems and pictures, but fostered the careers of a number of artists. On the ground floor of Potsdamer Strasse 134a were three narrow rooms in which the writer Lothar Schreyer, visiting them for the first time in 1911, found 'the fulfillment of all (his) artistic hopes.' In them could be found paintings by Jacoba van Heemskerck, Heinrich Campendonk and Franz Marc, the originator with Wassily Kandinsky, of the *Blaue Reiter* (Blue Rider) group of artists, an offshoot of *Die Brücke*—a group formed in Dresden in 1905 by three young architectural students, Ernst Ludwig Kirchner, Erich Heckel and Karl Schmidt-Rottluf.

'Weimar style,' as one writer put it, 'was born before the Weimar Republic.' And with innovations such as the introduction of psychoanalysis (the Berlin branch of the International Psychoanalytical Association was founded in 1910), with Max Reinhardt already an established producer and director, Arnold Schönberg having already broken through to atonality by 1912, the promise of the future seemed infinite. The writer Gerhart Hauptmann wrote of the beginning of the century: 'At the basis of our existence and life at that time was faith. We believed in the irresistible progress of humanity. We believed in the triumph of science and therefore in the ultimate unveiling of nature. . . .'

And Frederick Ewen wrote: 'Could any German be blamed if, say in the year 1914, looking back upon the preceding 35 years, he gloated over the catalog of distinguished names that marked the achievements of his country in so many fields; in science, medicine, history, political economy, archaeology, and letters? Names like Georg Cantor, Heinrich Hertz, Wilhelm Ostwald, Max Planck, Albert Einstein, Paul Ehrlich, Robert Koch, Leopold von Ranke, Theodor Mommsen, Julius Wellhausen, Karl Lamprecht, Karl Kautsky, Max Weber, Franz Mehring?'

The days of infinite promise were, however, numbered. The year 1913 was the twenty-fifth anniversary of the accession of Kaiser Wilhelm II. Amid the elaborate celebrations of national greatness there were a few discordant voices, one or two Cassandras who saw dark clouds on the horizon. The political scientist and industrialist Walther Rathenau warned of 'insolence gone mad' and the poet Frank Wedekind, in a poem written late in 1913 prophesied that 'Before a year is gone, this graveyard peace will end.' On 28 June 1914 the Austrian Archduke Francis Ferdinand was assassinated by a Serb nationalist in the Bosnian city of Sarajevo, and on 2 August the First World War began, almost simultaneous declarations having been made by France, Germany and Russia.

The outbreak of war was greeted with wild enthusiasm throughout the country. The atmosphere in Berlin was captured by the actress, Tilla Durieux, who recorded that there were 'Groups of people everywhere, and in addition, soldiers marching out of the city, showered with blossoms as they went. Every face looks happy: We've got war! Bands in the cafes and restaurants play *Heil dir im Siegerkranz* and *Die Wacht am Rhein* without stopping, and everybody has to listen to them standing up. . . . Soldiers at the railway stations are offered mountains of buttered sandwiches, sausages, and chocolate. There's a superabundance of everything: of people, of food, and of enthusiasm!'

Within a year disillusion set in. Soaring food prices and fading dreams of a swift German victory produced widespread and sometimes vociferous, discontent—in the summer of 1915 500 Berlin housewives stood in front of the Reichstag building, complaining about high prices and calling for their husbands' return from the front. They were hastily dispersed by the Prussian police and their gesture was not mentioned in the Berlin press.

The Reichstag could not, in any case, have done a great deal to help them, for its deputies, under the constitution framed by Bismarck, had been left virtually politically castrated—they could approve legislation put before them by the upper house, but not initiate it. The Emperor appointed his own Chancellor, who in his turn appointed his own carefully selected ministers of state, and no approval from the Reichstag was needed before treaties were signed, war declared or peace made. And if at any stage its deputies became intractable it was constitutionally within the Emperor's power to dissolve the Reichstag and call for new elections.

So, when on 2 August 1914 the Imperial Chancellor, Count von Bethmann-Hollweg, stood before Reichstag representatives and asked them to approve war credits of five million marks in order to finance the war, he both hoped

for and expected a majority vote in favor of this scheme. In the event he obtained it, but this time there had been an element of risk, since after the elections of 1912, the Reichstag had contained an unusually large rogue faction. In that year the Social Democratic party, 'the official voice of German socialism' had been returned in a position of some strength—110 members out of a total representation of 397, thus making it the largest single party in the Reichstag. The 'official position' of the Social Democratic party was Marxist and its attitude towards capitalism one of unconcealed dislike—under it, they threatened, the proletariat would get only 'mounting insecurity, misery, pressure, subordination, debasement and exploitation.'

Not surprisingly Bismarck had been vigorously opposed to the Social Democrats and passed laws which, until they lapsed in 1890, led to the imprisonment of 1500 socialists and the banning of 150 newspapers. Until the war, when recruiting needs brought some relaxation, socialists were rigidly excluded from the Army's officer corps and they were 'totally divorced from the favor of the Kaiser,' who refused to have them in his presence at all.

The Socialist vote for war credits was virtually a unanimous one—only one member abstaining. Outward signs of unanimity, however, had never concealed from Social Democrats themselves the implacable divisions in their ranks, divisions which had always existed between the left, center and right wings of the party. By the turn of the century the center and right of the party had opted for a policy of gradual evolution rather than violent revolution

Left: The Kaiser Gallery, a shopping arcade, built by von Kyllmann and Heyden in 1869–73.
Below: Another example of street theater typical of interwar Berlin.

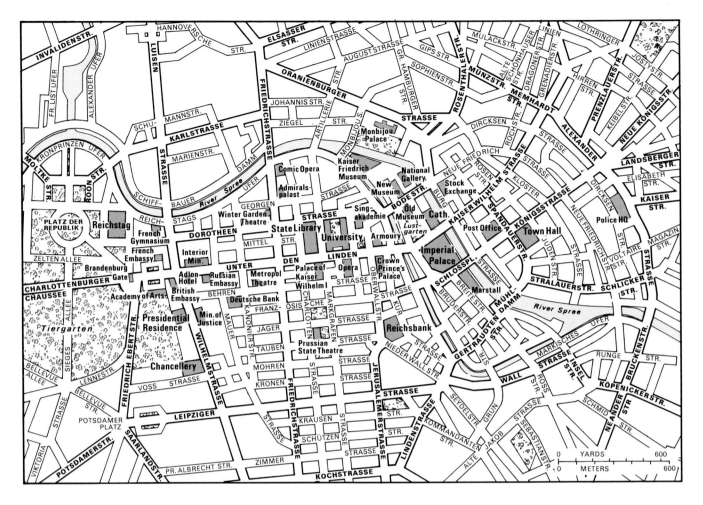

and the left, although ideologically opposed to this cautious revisionist view, were temporarily obliged to bow to the will of the majority.

German Social Democrats, however, cautiously reformist though they might be at home, had always jibbed at the idea of confronting their socialist brethren in the event of a European war. They believed with the Second International that such a war would amount only to 'workers shooting one another for the sake of capitalist profits.' It was common socialist policy to obstruct any such declaration and European socialist parties tacitly agreed that in the event of the outbreak of war they would vote against war credits, and so obstruct the financing of military mobilization. German Social Democrats justified their back-peddling on the grounds of personal weakness, national conscience and a belief in the Kaiser's protestations that Germany was fighting a 'defensive' war, with the expectation of attack and possible defeat by Russia, then considered 'the most reactionary power in Europe.'

Socialist consciences began to experience a twinge of disquiet when, after repelling the Russian attack, the German army turned its attention to conquering neutral Belgium and invading France, and socialist workers were seen to be dying for what began to look suspiciously like imperialist and capitalist reasons. In 1915, when asked to approve a further supply of war credits, the Social Democrats split (66 in favor and 44 against). By 1916 the party was irrevocably divided, eighteen deputies having formed what became known as the 'Independent Social Democratic Party,' the remainder calling themselves 'Majority Social-

ists.' The Independent Socialists contained such giants of the left as the theorist Eduard Bernstein, Karl Kautsky and Hugo Haase, the Majority Socialists 'old stalwarts and party officials' like Friedrich Ebert, Philipp Scheidemann, Eduard David and Gustav Noske.

The Independent Socialists attacked their rivals as 'opportunists, revisionists and traitors' and called for a return to fundamental socialist principles, the Majority Socialists retaliated with cries for unity: 'The danger which threatens the party is great! . . . Close the ranks!' The Independent Socialists had, however, attached to their ranks a small but ruthlessly militant and increasingly active group, the *Gruppe Internationale*. Their leader was a bespectacled lawyer who had already served a prison sentence for high treason—a former Reichstag deputy, expelled for his extreme views by the Majority Socialists— Karl Liebknecht; their theorist was a slight, 45-year-old Russian-Polish woman, a convinced anti-revisionist and revolutionary, whose tract *Guiding Principles* became the acknowledged blueprint for the group—Rosa Luxemburg.

As a result of huge German losses at Verdun and on the Somme, the Chief of the German General Staff, Erich von Falkenhayn, was dismissed by the Kaiser in the summer of 1916. He was replaced by two men—Field Marshal Paul von Hindenburg, who had the title of Chief of Staff, and General Erich Ludendorff, who had the title of Quartermaster-General, but who in effect became joint Chief of Staff. The Kaiser, who was temperamentally unable to bear bad news, had withdrawn almost completely among his entourage who knew better than to impart any. Having left Berlin at the beginning of the war to take up residence at army head-quarters, the Emperor had, in any case, become a shadowy figure, not seen by the people and had completely lost interest in the doings of the Reichstag, which he referred to as 'that monkey house.'

The Kaiser's vacillation and evasiveness paved the way for what amounted to a military dictatorship. Anxious to see an end to the war the Reichstag, including both Independent and Majority Socialists, threw itself firmly behind the two Chiefs of Staff. Gruppe Internationale, however, already impatient with the Independent Socialists' hot and cold attitude to the war, had decided to act independently. They changed their name to Spartakusbund (Spartacus Union), and began printing and distributing inflammatory leaflets calling for an end to 'the vile crime of nation murdering.' A mass demonstration organized by Lieb-knecht in Berlin in April 1916 calling for 'peace, bread and freedom' attracted 10,000 people, but it resulted in Lieb-knecht's arrest, trial and imprisonment, and the loss of his Reichstag seat. Three months later Rosa Luxemburg was jailed 'on no specific charge.'

As the war dragged on the miseries of civilians at home and soldiers at the front became more intense. The suffering caused by the allied blockade was acute. During the winter of 1916-17 there was a potato shortage and Germans were forced to eat turnips instead. The following year the weekly bread ration was reduced to seventy ounces and fat to two ounces per person. At the front it was as bad. 'The soldiers were so hungry,' wrote one historian, 'that they were stealing barley issued for horse fodder, grinding it up in their coffee mills and baking crude pancakes from it.'

The decay of Imperial Germany and the birth of the Weimar Republic followed one upon another with an almost Wagnerian inevitability. By the late summer of 1918 General Ludendorff was forced to face the unpalatable fact that nothing short of an overwhelming German victory would restore morale at home and at the front and that without it the war was lost. On 26 September the Allies launched a massive offensive between the Argonne and the Meuse, and with it all hopes of victory disappeared. Ludendorff broke down completely, screamed hysterically at everyone in sight and blamed the Reichstag for the way things had gone. Washing his hands of all further re-sponsibility he left them with the unenviable task of nego-tiating an armistice, obtaining an 'honest peace.'

And so, ironically, during the last few weeks of the war Germany achieved by chance what she had never achieved by effort, her 'first truly parliamentary and democratic government.' On 3 October Prince Max of Baden, a first cousin of the Kaiser, became Imperial Chancellor after the Supreme Command's puppet Chancellor, Count von Hertling, had resigned in desperation at the sudden down-turn of events. The secretaries of state were all ministers of the largest political parties. The Majority Socialists joined the government 'after much soul searching.' The Independent Socialists were not asked, 'nor would they have agreed to.' As Richard Watt put it: 'They saw with perfect clarity that the German Empire was on the edge of collapse, a prospect that did not dismay them. As the Em-pire foundered, the German Revolution would inevitably take place. All they had to do was stand aside and wait.'

They did not have to wait long. At the end of October, in the old Hanseatic port of Kiel on the Baltic sea, some sailors of the High Seas Fleet, having endured months of enforced idleness and lack of food, and having suddenly been ordered to put to sea in a last-ditch attempt to defeat the British Navy, became exasperated beyond endurance and mutinied. The ringleaders were arrested and im-prisoned, but the poison had already spread. On 3 Novem-ber 20,000 men poured into Kiel, bent on 'rescuing their comrades, restricting the power of their officers and forming workers' and sailors' councils.'

The harassed Reichstag deputies had more to come. Four hundred thousand munitions workers in Berlin went on strike, calling for 'peace, bread and freedom.' The allies were demanding peace terms which included the resigna-tion of the German government and the abdication of the Kaiser. The Kaiser, however, was obdurate. He had no intention of abdicating, neither did he see any necessity for it. To stave off the situation he fled from his palace at Potsdam to Spa in Belgium, where he joined the Supreme Command's headquarters. To crown it all, on 23 October Karl Liebknecht had been released from prison under a general amnesty, to be greeted in Berlin by a rapturous crowd and was pulled through the streets in a flower-filled carriage.

On 9 November a general strike was planned in Berlin, organized by the Independent Socialists and Spartacists

Below: Rosa Luxemburg, who was killed during the Spartacist Uprising in Berlin in 1919.

Top left: Communist demonstrators are dispersed by Berlin police in 1919.

Top center: Guards in front of the Ulanen Barracks warn their 'brothers,' fellow soldiers and workers, not to shoot during the November Uprising in 1918.

Above: Declaration of the establishment of the Republic from the balcony of the Crown Prince's Palace on 9 November 1918.

Left: Soldiers and workers cheer the November Revolution of 1918 which overthrew the Kaiser and established the Republic.

Above: Food distribution in the Reichstag.

Above: Popular support for the revolutionaries.

and designed to bring about the abdication of the Kaiser and the dissolution of the monarchy. By mid-morning large crowds had gathered in front of the Reich Chancellery brandishing red flags and shouting slogans. 'Entire military units,' wrote one commentator, 'even such elite ones as the Tsar Alexander Guards Regiment joined the demonstrators. Hundreds of thousands of Berlin workers and their wives, as well as soldiers and sailors, streamed

Below: Members of the People's Naval Division occupy a government building in December 1918.

into the city center where Government offices clustered. Crack units such as the Naumburg Rifles sent in to protect Government buildings, "went over to the people" and individual soldiers placed on guard by the Government either quit their posts or simply let the revolutionaries stream by. . . .'

Eventually the leader of the Majority Socialists, Friedrich Ebert, a former saddlemaker, led a delegation of his party to see Prince Max of Baden. He said that 'for the preservation of peace and order . . . we regard it as indispensable that the office of imperial chancellor and the Brandenburg

command be held by members of our party.' Prince Max could only agree, his government disintegrating before his very eyes and the army and the navy in confusion. Philipp Scheidemann, the only other Social Democrat in the cabinet, then opened a window of the Reichstag and shouted to the crowd below that Ebert was now Chancellor, adding 'Long live the German Republic' (much to the fury of Ebert, who found that on top of everything else he was faced with an invalid constitution).

Later in the day the Chancellor was able to establish in a private telephone conversation with General Gröner, then Quartermaster-General, that the High Command would support his new regime so long as it resisted 'Bolshevism' (tacitly understood by them both to be a euphemism for 'any social change'). General Gröner also revealed that the Kaiser had finally been persuaded by his own generals that the day's events in Berlin had left him no choice but to abdicate, and he had gone into self-imposed exile in Holland.

There was, however, another revolution in Berlin that day. The same afternoon Karl Liebknecht walked into the Imperial Palace, over which a red flag was already flying, and from a balcony proclaimed 'the free Socialist Republic of Germany which shall comprise all Germans.' The army barracks was occupied by a soldiers' council, the police headquarters by some members of the extreme left wing of the Independents, and the offices of the Conservative newspaper *Lokal-Anzeiger* were taken over by Spartacists who, supervised by Rosa Luxemburg, recently released from prison, used their equipment to print their own paper, *Die Rote Fahne* (The Red Flag).

The two revolutions existed side by side for a short time, but the Spartacists were essentially anti-war, and, after the armistice of 11 November, the impetus for their uprising dwindled. Their activities, however, had created a common front for Chancellor Ebert and General Gröner, who determined to rid themselves of their turbulent rivals. After the armistice the German army was dispersed—two million men were evacuated from France, Belgium, Luxembourg, Alsace-Lorraine and the German Rhineland in 31 days—under the terms of the agreement, 'any German troops remaining in the area after one month would be taken prisoner by the advancing Allies.'

The German army, however, was not so easily disintegrated. Many officers, deprived not only of their livelihood but of their raison d'être, formed volunteer groups under the overall direction of the Minister of Defense, Gustav Noske, but raised and organized by General Georg von Maercker. These 'various little armies' became known as the 'Freikorps.'

And when on Sunday 5 January 1919 a mass demonstration took place in front of the police headquarters, protesting at the replacement of the left-wing independent Police President Emil Eichhorn by one more sympathetic to the Ebert government, it was the Freikorps who were called upon to restore order to Berlin.

It was by no means an easy task. The Spartacists, occupying the building and taken aback by the size and enthusiasm of the crowd outside, allowed themselves to be convinced that their hour had come. They decided to 'call a general strike, to support an armed attack upon the Government and to place Germany in the vanguard of the international

Above: Freikorps tank patrols Berlin streets in 1919.

proletarian revolution.' Rosa Luxemburg, however, was not so convinced and urged restraint. Only the week before she had written in *Die Rote Fahne*: 'It would be a criminal error to seize power now. The German working class is not ready for such an act.'

Ready or not they were aroused. The Revolutionary Committee distributed arms, riflemen were stationed on top of the Brandenburg Gate, and on the 6th the general strike began. 'Bourgeois' newspaper offices were seized, as was the Government Printing Office, some railway stations and a large brewery. Count Harry Kessler, a poet and diplomat and an indefatigable diarist of the Weimar Republic, described the scene in Berlin on 6 January: 'Eleven o'clock, corner of Siegesallee and Viktoriastrasse. Two processions meet, the one is going in the direction of Siegesallee, the other in that of Wilhelmstrasse. They are made up of . . . artisans and factory girls . . . waving the same red flags and moving in the same sort of shambling step. But they carry slogans, jeer at each other as they pass, and perhaps will be shooting one another down before the day is out.'

The Majority Socialists, flustered and intimidated, turned to the remnants of the army for help and asked Colonel Reinhard, then in the process of forming a Berlin Freikorps, to expel the Spartacists from the newspaper offices they held. Delighted to have something on which to cut their teeth, the various bands of Freikorps went to work with a will. They gave their adversaries one chance to surrender and then began firing trench mortars and machine guns at the *Vorwärts* offices, throwing grenades through the windows and burning down the back of the building with flamethrowers—turning a conveniently blind eye to the white flags soon waved by the overpowered Spartacists.

It was a pattern the Freikorps, who were increased in strength to over 3000, were able to repeat again and again. Karl Liebknecht and Rosa Luxemburg went into hiding, but on 15 January were discovered in the flat of one of Liebknecht's relatives in the Berlin-Wilmersdorf district. They were taken to the nearby Eden Hotel 'for questioning,' during the course of which they were beaten. Later they were each knocked unconscious by a blow from a rifle butt, bundled into separate cars and driven away. Liebknecht was taken to the Tiergarten, allowed out of the car and then

Right: Freikorps troops armed with machine guns patrol the Dom area in January 1919.
Center right: Communist demonstrators in Munich mourn the death of the two Spartacist leaders in Berlin, Karl Liebknecht and Rosa Luxemburg. Munich was in Communist hands twice during 1918–19 until the Freikorps crushed them.
Far right: Barricade of government troops in Berlin during January 1919.
Below right: Elections for the National Assembly which drafted the Weimar Constitution took place on 19 January 1919.

shot dead. Rosa Luxemburg was shot through the head in the car, and her body then thrown from the Liechtenstein bridge into the Landwehr canal.

Chancellor Ebert professed himself 'horrified' by the murders, but despite his protestations of disgust the killers of the two Communist leaders escaped with insultingly light sentences: one, Lieutenant Vogel, convicted of 'failing to report a death' and of 'illegally disposing of a corpse,' managed to make his escape to Holland on a forged passport; the other, Private Bunge, accused of 'attempted manslaughter,' served a token few months in prison.

There was an aftermath of bizarre logicality. Amid what Richard Watt described as 'the still-smoldering wreckage of the Spartacist Week uprising,' national elections were held, (although, not surprisingly, they were boycotted by the Communists). The result of this eminently sensible measure was a massive success for the Majority Socialists, who obtained 39 percent of the popular vote, winning 163 out of a possible 423, thus becoming the largest single party in the government.

To dissociate itself from the militaristic and monarchic associations of Berlin and Potsdam, the new régime turned to the little town of Weimar, home of Goethe and Schiller, in the hope that it, as the embodiment of humanitarianism and liberalism, would provide an 'auspicious birthplace' for the new German constitution.

On 24 February the National Assembly met in the old national theater of Weimar to deliberate the draft constitution drawn up by Hugo Preuss. It was, as A J P Taylor commented, the 'most mechanically perfect of all democratic constitutions, full of admirable devices—parliamentary sovereignty, the referendum, the most elaborate and perfect system of proportional representation ever conceived—a textbook constitution for the Professor of Political Science.' It did, however, contain one flaw. Article 48 decreed that the President of the 'Reich' (as the German nation was now to be called) could intervene whenever 'the public safety and order in the German Reich were seriously disturbed or endangered.'

With hindsight, its misuse seems only too inevitable. But what after all could one expect, as Professor Craig pointed out, of 'the ordinary German, when a Thomas Mann could say in 1918: "I don't want the trafficking of Parliament and parties that leads to the infection of the whole body of the nation with the virus of politics . . . I don't want politics. I want impartiality, order, and propriety. If that is Philistine, then I want to be a Philistine."' It was not, as he also said, 'a very good foundation for a democratic republic.'

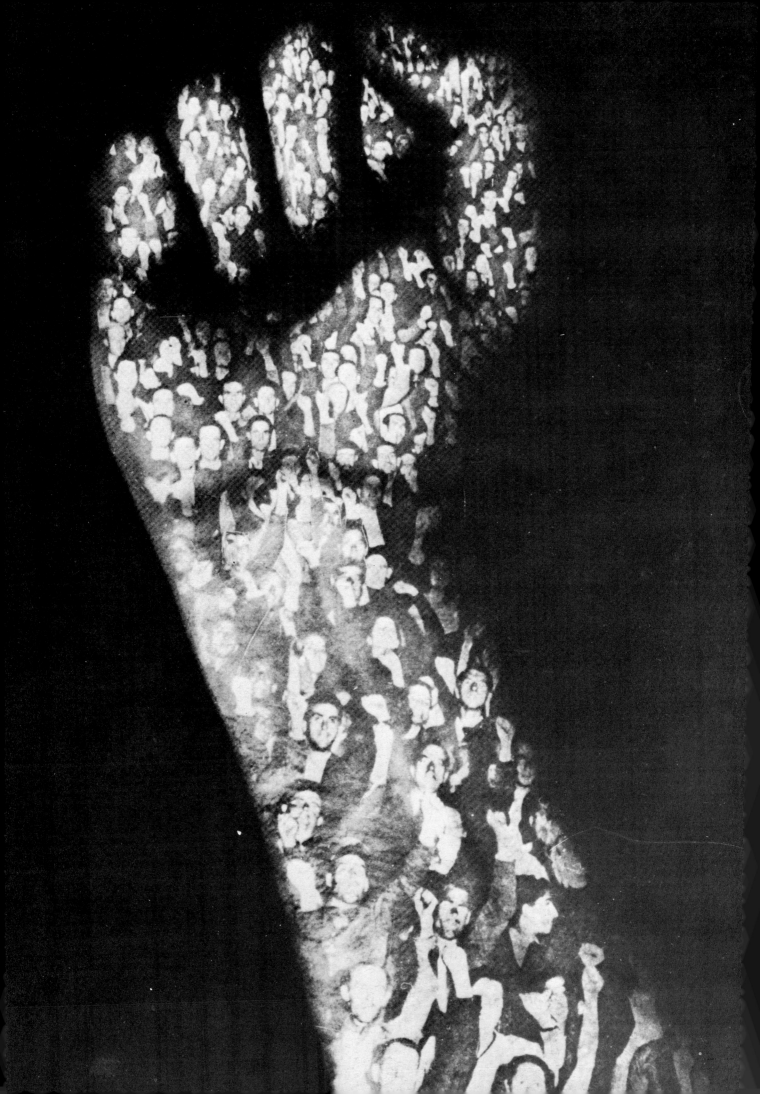

BAUHAUSSTADT

John Heartfield's photomontage of the workers united in the
fight against capitalism.

During the winter of 1922–23 the painter Lazlo Moholy-Nagy created a collage. It was called '25 Pleitegeier,' or 'The Bankruptcy Vultures,' and it was made not from plaster, paint and canvas, but from banknotes. As he explained, 'I roomed with Kurt Schwitters in an almost unheated attic studio in Spichernstrasse, Berlin. The German mark had reached an inflammatory value of 25 million. We had no money to buy paint and canvas. So Kurt inspired me to follow his example and use the "currency" of the day to make collages.'

Lazlo Moholy-Nagy was the victim, with many others, of the crippling effect of inflation, which between 1919 and 1923 saw the value of the German mark decline from the prewar level against the dollar of 4.2 to 4,200,000,000,000. Under the Treaty of Versailles, signed on Saturday 28 June 1919 in the Hall of Mirrors (where in 1871 Wilhelm I had been proclaimed Emperor) Germany had been brought to her knees. The Allies demanded and got the total renouncement of her colonial empire, of one-eighth of her territory annexed in previous wars of conquest, lands which included Alsace-Lorraine, Schleswig-Holstein and the Saar, and (to further satisfy the Allies) a fifteen-year occupation of the Rhineland; the reduction of her army, then still 500,000 strong, to a paltry 96,000 men and 4000 officers, and reparations in excess of five billion dollars—considered small enough payment for the 'cost of sunken Allied merchant vessels . . . pensions to disabled soldiers' and 'the restoration of devastated France.'

Such draconian measures on the part of the allies were bound to have repercussions. Those that followed might have been foreseen, it has been pointed out. The humiliation of such an 'agreement' came as an outright surprise to Germans, who for four years had been deluded that they were winning the war, and had then been lulled into believing that they would obtain an honorable peace.

Philipp Scheidemann, then Chancellor, cried melodramatically, 'May the hand wither that signs such a treaty!' and then resigned when he saw there was no alternative but to comply with allied demands. Gustav Bauer, the Social Democrat who formed a new government in the subsequent elections, was not so squeamish, neither was his eminently realistic Vice-Chancellor, Matthias Erzberger, who stressed repeatedly that, 'When one signs under duress there is no question of insincerity.'

The treaty was, nevertheless, an anathema to the army and especially to the Freikorps, many of whom, when told they must disband, refused point blank. One such was the crack Second Marine Brigade of Captain Hermann Ehrhardt, with the result that 3000 troops from this brigade, together with 2000 from some Baltic Freikorps, marched on Berlin. There they attempted to install 'an obscure nationalist civil servant named Wolfgang Kapp' as Chan-

Below: From left to right: President Wilson, Premier Clemenceau, Lord Balfour and Premier Orlando attending the Paris Peace Conference in 1919.

cellor and take over the running of the country. This military insurrection was not entirely unexpected, but nevertheless created a great deal of alarm. Cabinet Ministers fled to Dresden, where General von Maercker threatened to put them all under arrest. The *putsch*, however, was a failure—mainly on account of the inadequacy of Wolfgang Kapp—but also due to the 'astonishing effectiveness' of a general strike called by the Socialists to bring about his downfall. Kapp was eventually obliged to flee the country, but the Freikorps were more difficult to get rid of—they lingered on in various guises and remained a constant thorn in the flesh of the Weimar Republic.

The exorbitant reparations demanded by the allies undoubtedly contributed heavily to the downward slide of the mark. But the Kapp *Putsch* and on 24 June 1922 the brutal assassination of the brilliant and talented Foreign Minister, Walther Rathenau, at the hands of a right-wing anti-Semite contributed to the general sense of instability and brought the always sensitive money market to a state of panic and confusion. All security had gone; there was no gold, no standard, no hope of economic recovery. The slogan 'work is salvation' became a bitter irony as the unemployment figures soared to fresh heights, and even if work was to be found the 'reward for honest living was now worth less money.' As one writer put it, 'In the end, a worker needed a shopping bag to carry one day's miserable wages to the grocer. And thrifty, middle-class Germans carted their life savings to the butcher or baker in wheelbarrows.'

Above: Scheidemann (second from the left) greets soldiers returning to Berlin in December 1918.

The degradation of the poor and the cynicism of the republican government, which was later accused of prolonging inflation in order to avoid reparations, deeply influenced a number of left-wing artists working in Berlin at that time. The caricaturist George Grosz was one. A card-carrying member of the Communist Party (given to him in 1919 by Rosa Luxemburg herself) he trod a strongly individualistic path, presenting a highly satirical view of the ills of society. When he became disillusioned with the

Below left: Philipp Scheidemann announces the terms of Versailles to the Berlin crowd in May 1919.
Below: Election time in 1928.

Above: Communist party supporters campaign for the Reichstag election in 1924.
Right: Pro-Kapp troops set up their positions near the Brandenburg Gate during the putsch of 1920.
Far right: Members of the Ehrhardt Brigade in Berlin.

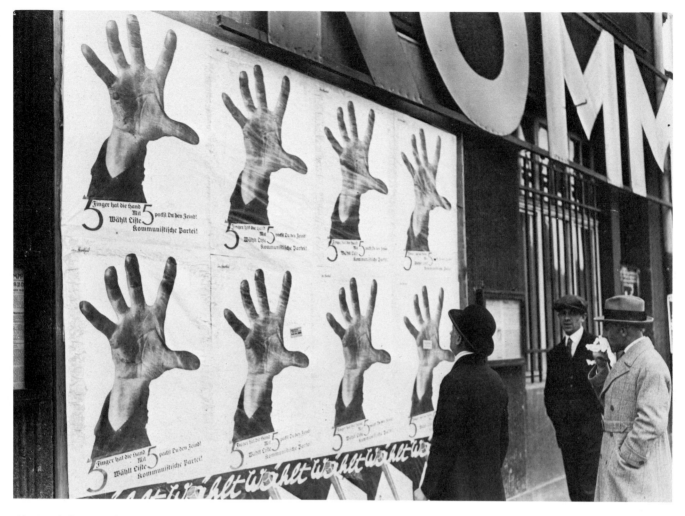

Above: A Communist wall poster by John Heartfield in 1928. During the heyday of the Weimar Republic the Communists were particularly strong in 'Red Berlin.'

Communist Party, after the failure of the Spartacist rising, he became more conscious of the artist's role as a moralist. In 1925 he said 'The realist holds up a mirror for his contemporaries so that they can see their own faces. I drew and painted from contradictions and I tried to persuade the world through my art that it is ugly, sick and a liar.' At first Grosz defined the class enemy as the prominent members of the ruling class: 'the burghers and the aristocrats and the militarists and the judges,' but in the late Twenties he caricatured the bourgeoisie and the petty-bourgeois more virulently.

Ernst Gombrich once commented that the 'dangerous, virtually magical element in caricature' is the ability 'to copy a person, to mimic his behavior' and, in so doing, 'to annihilate his individuality'—and in his work for *Malik Verlag*, the journal founded by the writer Wieland Herzfelde and his brother John Heartfield after the First World War, Grosz did just that. He produced painful, biting and cruelly derisive portfolios of drawings, attacking soldiers (*Gott mit uns*, published in 1920), capitalists (*Im Schatten*, published 1921) and the ruling class (*Das Gesicht der herrschende Klasse*, published 1921).

In them he attacks the survival of militarism in the Weimar Republic and also capitalist exploitation. To make his point, Grosz represented the class struggle in socicty in dialectical images and thus propagated his Marxist views.

Grosz was a prey to the contradictions of the day: rebellion and adaptation. He felt bound to attack the injustices around him. The fortunes made during the period of inflation were particularly repulsive to Grosz—the industrialist Hugo Stinnes became a special target for his vitriolic pen.

Even more traitorous than the capitalists in the eyes of most Communists were the sycophants who betrayed their socialist brethren by obsequious toadying to their masters. Rosa Luxemburg, in a handbill issued by the Spartacus League, compared them to 'a dog who licks the boots of his master for serving him with kicks for many years,' and Grosz, in a savage portfolio entitled *Abrechnung Folgt*, illustrated this theme—the cover drawing showed a fat figure licking a large, shiny military boot. The workers themselves, on the other hand, obtained sympathetic if unsentimental treatment; they were shown as being oppressed and deprived through no fault of their own—thin, stooping figures in shapeless clothes, resignedly marching to work or sitting glumly on benches, alternately ignored, exploited or abused by their tormentors.

But by far the most popular exponent of popular realism was Heinrich Zille, who was to Berlin what Théophile Daumier had been to Paris, 'the observer of grim humor and strange beauty in the city's deprivation and decay.' After he had been made a member of the Berlin Academy, the right-wing newspaper *Fridericus* reported disgustedly, 'The Berlin portrayer of toilets and pregnancy, Heinrich

Above: A caricature of Berliners drawn by George Grosz.
Above right: Grosz in his atelier in 1928.
Right: Grosz with Rudolf Grossman (left) in 1932.
Below right: Grosz tries his hand at the banjo in 1927.
Below: Grosz and Wieland Herzfelde (left) on trial in one of the many cases brought against the painter for obscenity.

Below: Germany's fastest streamliner leaves Berlin's Tegel
Railway Yard on its first trial. It raced at 175 km (over
100 mph).
Opposite: Traffic in the Pariserplatz on the birthday of
President von Hindenburg in 1926.

05 001

Left: John Heartfield's poster explains 'The meaning of the Hitler salute: the little man begs for great gifts.'
Above: Heartfield's photomontage caricaturing Hindenburg.
Below left: Otto Dix in 1928.
Below: Grosz's *Barricades* and other works on show.

Zille, has become a member of the Academy of Arts and has been approved by the minister.—Cover your face, O Muse!'

Another more humane observer of the poor was Käthe Kollwitz, described by one art historian as 'one of the most powerfully emotional German artists of this century.' A pacifist—one of her sons was killed in 1914—and a Communist (although disillusioned after a trip to Russia in 1927), and married to a Berlin doctor, she dedicated herself to stirring the consciences of the rich by tugging at their heart strings. (Her lithographs of the Mother and Child won acclaim before the First World War, but the Kaiser refused her the gold medal awarded by the Academy of Arts for the transparent reason that he resented her 'probing the human shadows of his empire.')

The daily meeting place for artists in Berlin was the Cafe des Westens on the corner of the Kurfürstendamm and the Joachimsthalerstrasse, nicknamed by those in the know the 'Cafe Megalomania.' Ernst Blass described it in the days before the First World War: 'I still remember the cafe in all-powerful Berlin. The drowsy gaslight. Lots of people with determined faces. Newspapers and waiters. Just as it ought to be. . . . What was in the air? Above all Van Gogh, Nietzsche, Freud too, and Wedekind. Van Gogh stood for Expression and experience as opposed to

Impressionism and Naturalism. Flaming concentration, youthful sincerity, immediacy, depth; exhibition and hallucination. The term Expressionism had been coined by others; but in our circle we had been sailing in Expressionistic waters for a long time. (It) meant the courage of one's own means of expression; the courage to be oneself. . . .'

But which self? That was the confusing thing. Futurist? Extreme Expressionistic? Constructivist? Dadaist? Otto Dix was one of the artists working in Berlin who explored the new objectivity or realism. His meticulous paintings did not attack society as Grosz's did but allowed the spectator to make his own judgment on the painting's subject. He wrote 'it has always been a matter of major importance to me to come as close as possible to that which I am observing. For more important than the "how" is the "what." Only from the "what" can the "how" emerge.'

Neither of these concepts troubled the Dadaists. Expressionism, Futurism and Cubism were swept away in the frenzy of anarchic glee and in their place was put Dadaism. The childish connotations of the word—said to have been found by chance by Hugo Ball and Richard Hülsenbeck in a German-French dictionary—were apt. In French it was defined as 'hobby-horse,' and in German 'an indication of idiot naivety and of an (sic) preoccupation with procreation and the baby carriage.' Dada was infantile, but it did not have the infant's capacity for growth and change; it was primitive but it had no innocence; it was an artistic game without any rules, and it sprang from, and ultimately died in, confusion. 'What we call Dada,' wrote Hugo Ball in a letter dated 28 November 1916 to his friend Richard Hülsenbeck, 'is foolery extracted from the emptiness in which all the higher problems are wrapped, a gladiator's gesture, a game played without the shabby remnants . . . a public execution of false morality.'

The movement was born in Zurich in a bar called the Meierei where the 'philosopher, novelist, cabaret performer, journalist and mystic,' Hugo Ball, persuaded the proprietor, a Herr Ephraim, to allow him to conduct a 'literary cabaret.' Herr Ephraim had, however, some reservations about the strange entertainment provided by his odd clients. Their cabaret, which Ball christened the Cabaret Voltaire, contained such baffling items as the sculptor Hans Arp 'tearing up bits of paper, letting them fall onto a board, and gluing them down wherever they fell'; the Rumanian poet Tristan Tzara either reading his own poems in Rumanian or just making them up at random from newspaper clippings; Hugo Ball's mistress (later his wife), Emmy Hennings, reciting poems or singing provocative songs in her high, shrill, clear voice; and the physician, poet and painter, Richard Hülsenbeck, declaiming his 'Phantastische Gebete' (Fantastic Prayers) to the accompaniment of 'a rhythmically swishing riding crop,' or a negro-inspired beating of the tomtom.

When Dada reached Berlin after the First World War it took on a different, sharper complexion. For Berlin, unlike Zurich, had actually lived through a real war, had suffered a real revolution and was in a real state of depression. Zurich (despite the fact that Lenin lived in lodgings opposite the Cabaret Voltaire) remained a city of ideas and dreams, a comfortable retreat from the turmoil of the rest of

Prolet, wie lange noch? Wirf ab das Hakenjoch!

Keine Stimme den Faschisten oder Stinnessozialisten. Kämpfe mit den Kommunisten!

Above: A Communist poster claiming that the proletariat had labored long enough under the yoke of the swastika and should vote for the Social Democrats.

Europe. George Grosz, involved in the beginnings of the German Dada movement, wrote: 'The German Dada movement had its roots in the perception that came to some of my comrades and to me at the same time, that it was complete nonsense to believe that spirit or anything spiritual ruled the world. Goethe in bombardments; Nietzsche in knapsacks; Jesus in trenches. But there were still people who thought spirit and art had power. . . . Dada was not an ideological movement, but an organic product which arose as a reaction to the cloud-wandering tendencies of the so-called sacred art which found meaning in cubes and gothic, while the field commanders painted in blood.'

Richard Hülsenbeck came to Berlin from Zurich, as did Raoul Hausmann and Franz Jung, the publishers of the anarchistic journal, *Die Freie Strasse*. The gallery of the art dealer J B Neuemann became a substitute for the Cabaret Voltaire, with Hülsenbeck reading his Fantastic Prayers and George Grosz 'performing an obscene tap dance in which he relieved himself in pantomine before a Louis Corinth painting'—an act too brazen even for that enlightened audience, 'which literally rose in disgust.' Richard Hülsenbeck wrote a manifesto for Dada which was read in the Neue Sezession hall in Berlin on 12 April 1919. It began on a high-flown note: 'Art in its execution and direction is dependent on the time in which it lives, and artists are creatures of their epoch. The highest art will be that which in its conscious content presents the thousand-fold problems of the day . . . the best and most extraordinary artists will be those who every hour snatch the tatters of their bodies out of the frenzied cataract of life, who, with bleeding hands and hearts, hold fast to the intelligence of their time,' and ended on a more down-to-earth one: 'Blast the aesthetic-ethical attitude! Blast the bloodless abstraction of expressionism! Blast the literary hollowheads and their theories for improving the world! For Dadaism in word and image, for all the Dada things that go on in the world! To be against this manifesto is to be a Dadaist!'

Dada was officially launched at last and with it the Club Dada, for as the manifesto stressed, 'Dada is a CLUB, founded in Berlin, which you can join without commitments. In this club every man is president and every man can have his say in artistic matters.' Many did—in an orgy of artistic license young artists jumped on the bandwagon of free expression and set out to 'épater les bourgeois.' One, Kurt Schwitters, spent his time, according to Otto Friedrich, 'pasting together collages of old bus tickets, cloakroom stubs, buttons, inner tubes and pieces of string,' and feeling the need for a larger canvas, extended his mania to the walls of his house, and even to the rooms themselves, which became full to overflowing with ephemera, which he solemnly described as 'freestanding objects.' He also composed a very humorous Dada poem; Merz Number 1, Anna Blume:

Anna Blume, o beloved one of my twenty-seven senses,
    I love you—
I you, you I, me you I, you you me—Us?
Never mind (in other words it's our affair)
Who are you, woman who has never been counted?
You are—are you? They say who you are—
let them say, they don't know how a steeple
stands upright. You carry your hat on your feet
and you wander on your hands, on your hands you
    wander.

In the nature of things Dadaists played a running game of cat and mouse with the authorities. Many of the Dada magazines, which included *Every Man His Own Football*, *The Bordello*, *Rose Colored Glasses* and *Bankrupt* were banned almost before they had seen the light of day. In July and August 1920 the First International Dada Fair was held in Berlin, which contained 174 blatantly political and antimilitaristic exhibits, accompanied by slogans such as 'Dada is political' and 'Dada fights on the side of the revolutionary proletariat.' Hanging from the ceiling in the central room was 'the stuffed effigy of a German officer with a pig's head . . . labelled "Hanged by the Revolution."' George Grosz's portfolio, *Gott mit uns*, was also prominently displayed.

Not unnaturally, officers visiting the exhibition were outraged, feeling it to be a deliberately provocative baiting of the officers and men of the Reichswehr. Copies of *Gott mit uns* were impounded on the instructions of the Berlin police president 'at the behest of the Reichswehr Ministry' and George Grosz as its creator, Wieland Herzfelde as its publisher and Rudolf Schlichter as the sculptor of the 'offensive effigy,' were committed for trial on charges of 'insulting members of the Reichswehr.' Both Grosz and

1927 Der Junggeselle Nr. 43
Nachdruck und öffentlicher Vortrag sämtlicher Beiträge verboten

1927 Der Junggeselle Nr. 38
Nachdruck und öffentlicher Vortrag sämtlicher Beiträge verboten

Herzfelde were fined respectively 300 and 600 marks (considered an almost disappointingly lenient verdict by some Dadaists, who were particularly annoyed with the defense line that the Fair and its exhibits were 'not meant seriously.'

Grosz, however, had to stand trial on two subsequent occasions, once in 1923 as a result of the publication of his masterpiece, the portfolio of drawings *Ecce Homo* when it was stated that 'a significant portion of the drawings offend the modesty and moral sense of the viewer in respect to sexual matters,' and more seriously in 1928 when he was arrested and tried on a charge of blasphemy after the publication of *Hintergrund*. After a sensational trial he was eventually acquitted of this charge, having managed to convince his jurors that the drawings were the outcome of a genuine aversion to warfare rather than a calculated act of profanity. Later, however, after an appeal by the public prosecutor, the drawings were confiscated, the reason given that they might 'be misunderstood and therefore give offense.'

Although Dadaism was the most bizarre artistic movement in Berlin in the early Twenties, it was not the only one to turn art into an instrument of revolution. The *Novembergruppe*, founded in 1918 by Max Pechstein, had similar but rather more soberly constructive aims. Among its members were the painters Lyonel Feininger and Emil Nolde, the sculptors Georg Kolbe and Gerhard Marcke, the architects Walter Gropius and Eric Mendelsohn, the art historians Paul Zucker and Wilhelm Valentiner, the art dealer Alfred Flechtheim together with the composers Kurt Weill and Paul Hindemith and the playwright Bertholt Brecht.

Like the Dadaists the *Novembergruppe* issued various high-minded manifestoes stating their aims. The first said

Above: Two cartoons from *Der Junggeselle*. Above left two girls are depicted on holiday in the sun; above an old gentleman is being seduced by a 'lady of the night.'

that 'The future of art and the seriousness of this hour forces us revolutionaries of the spirit (Expressionists, Cubists, Futurists) towards unity and close co-operation'; another addressed to 'all artists' extolled the virtue of all painters and poets being bound to the poor 'in a sacred solidarity,' crying: 'Will not the bourgeoisie soon again seize the reins of power through putsches, corruption, and unscrupulous vote manipulations? Will not this Germany of the conquering middle class once again make shameless use of the workers' strength and humble the poor even further?'

These questions were legitimate ones. The year 1924, however, saw the stabilization of the hitherto wildly inflating mark and a peaceful return to a reasonably ordered prosperity. In 1920 the Reparations Commission ordered Germany to pay 209 billion gold marks to the Allies over a period of 35 years. When it became apparent that there was no possibility of Germany complying with these overoptimistic demands, the Allies were forced to reduce the liability to 132 billion marks. Even so the Germans fell behind, and the French occupied the Ruhr in an attempt to enforce payment. 'Thereupon,' wrote Richard M Watt, 'Germany, partly by government design and partly because of faulty economic policies, was launched into a period of wild inflation, which ruined the German middle class and brought nothing appreciable to the allies in terms of reparations' payments.'

As a result of this impasse the German government itself and the United States took various measures under the Dawes Plan to stabilize the mark and finance reparations.

Above: Two children enjoy the horse racing at the Hoppegarten.
Above right: A brass band entertains the racegoers.
Opposite right: Ladies wear their best to go to the races at the Hoppegarten.
Extreme right: Hindenburg congratulates the winning jockey in the Hindenburg stakes run at the Hoppegarten.
Below: The parade at the horse show in Buckow.

The first spring run of the German Women's Automobile
Club from Berlin to the Mecklenburg Lake.

The value of the mark was linked to the value of land and America undertook to loan Germany a significant proportion of the money she needed to repay allied demands. In effect, as Richard Watt pointed out, 'Germany was permitted to borrow from all sides in vast amounts; at one period, 1924–31, she borrowed eighteen billion marks, while paying out only about eleven billion.'

However, the very simplicity of these arrangements and the speed with which they were implemented, fuelled middle class suspicions that they had lost everything for nothing and injected a dangerous air of cynicism and contempt for the government among the bankrupt and the unemployed. The government was attacked on all sides, on the left for betraying the revolution and on the right 'for fomenting it in the first place.'

The 1924 general elections had increased the number of right-wing nationalist members in the Reichstag to 103, making them the second largest faction after the Social Democrats, who had 131. And in 1925, with the death of Friedrich Ebert, the aging Field Marshal Hindenburg, candidate of the right wing, was elected President in his stead—a retrograde step seen by the allies as a sign that Germany had not yet rid herself of old nationalist and militaristic habits.

Despite an uneasy coalition between left and right in the Reichstag and despite the legacy of bankruptcy and unemployment left over from the years of inflation, Berlin enjoyed another boom from 1924 until 1929. The stabilization of the mark and the sight of British and American money pouring into the capital was an encouragement for foreign bankers to grant loans to German industrial enterprises. One or two empires, however, had crashed beyond all hope of resuscitation. The Ruhr coal baron, Hugo Stinnes, target of George Grosz's merciless pen and described by Count Harry Kessler as 'a cross between a patriarch, a commercial traveller and the Fying Dutchman,' died in the spring of 1924. His heirs had to bear the brunt of the losses which by 1925 had led to the liquidation of their empire. Another casualty was Barmat Enterprises, a foodstuffs' company, whose founder had established 'close links' with the new republican government. Through the Bank of Prussia he was granted extended loans which he was eventually unable to honor; credit was withdrawn and the company 'collapsed under a debt of ten billion marks.'

A side effect of the boom in Berlin during the mid-Twenties was the blossoming of new architectural projects which, if they did not change the face of imperial Berlin, were at least a welcome antidote to the prevailing grayness and solidity. Today Berlin is a city of light and glass, containing such exotica as Ludwig Mies van der Rohe's Gallery, Scharoun's Philharmonic Hall with its deliberately asymmetrical structure and its tent-like roof, Le Corbusier's apartment houses and the vast shell-shaped Congress Hall, resting on 2000 concrete supports, in which the acoustics are said to be so good that 'a speaker can be heard in every one of the 1264 seats without using a microphone.' But behind the open, tree-lined streets lie scores of cramped apartment blocks—gaunt reminders of prewar Berlin, for ironically the bombs that flattened the palaces and public buildings left many of these standing.

'Architecture,' wrote Ludwig Mies van der Rohe in 1923, 'is the will of an epoch translated into space,' a testament to which the early development of Berlin bore ample witness. In 1853 at the request of Frederick William IV, the Chief of Police drew up a city plan for Berlin in order to cater for the unmanageable influx of workers and soldiers into the city after the Napoleonic wars. Frederick expressly stated that he wanted 'to spend as little as possible for streets and parks to accommodate them.' As a result the Chief of Police produced a plan containing narrow streets and 'tightly packed seven-storey tenements with as many as five successive inner courts to provide a minimum of light and air.' Twenty years later, although the German Association of Architects demanded that these be pulled down and even Bismarck noted 'an increase in tenant revolts and health and sanitation problems,' very little was done.

Gerhard Masur in his book *Imperial Berlin* described the tenements as being 'built round courtyards, the connection between the rooms facing the street and those facing the courtyard . . . established through a gateway room lit by one large window opening on the courtyard. This usually dark and forbidding chamber served as the dining room. . . . Further along were bedrooms, bathroom, pantry and kitchen. Frequently the kitchen was at the very end of a dark corridor and a considerable distance from the dining room.' And Christopher Isherwood drew a vivid picture of the same sort of apartment block in the Wassertorstrasse, unchanged since the end of the nineteenth century, in his collection of stories *Goodbye to Berlin* published in 1939. It was in a 'deep shabby cobbled street, littered with sprawling children in tears' where 'lying in bed, in the darkness, in my tiny corner of the enormous human warren of the tenements, I could hear, with uncanny precision, every sound which came up from the courtyard below. The shape of the court must have acted as a gramophone-horn. . . . It was alien and mysterious and uncanny, like sleeping out in the jungle alone.'

A far cry from the damp, dark tenements of the working class were the suburban villas of the prosperous bourgeoisie. In the late nineteenth century the fashion in Grunewald and Charlottenburg was for elaborate replicas of Italian palaces; in the 1920s the rich turned to the new fashionable architects, Mies van der Rohe, Walter Gropius or Eric Mendelsohn for their individually designed status symbols.

Nineteenth-century public buildings were massive and elaborate. The court architect, Ernst von Ihne, was responsible for the Kaiser Friedrich Museum and also for the new Royal Library on the Unter den Linden, built just before the First World War in seventeenth-century style; at the turn of the century Ludwig Hofman created the museum for the Mark Brandenburg, described as 'a curious combination of church, city hall, tower, and patrician mansion.' As Gerhard Masur commented, 'The public buildings of the second empire in Berlin were at best tradition-bound; at worst copies of famous models which they could not hope to equal.'

There were, however, some fresh elements at work. Hermann Muthesius, a young architect, was sent to London in 1896 as the official representative of the Prussian Board of Trade in order to report on British architecture and design.

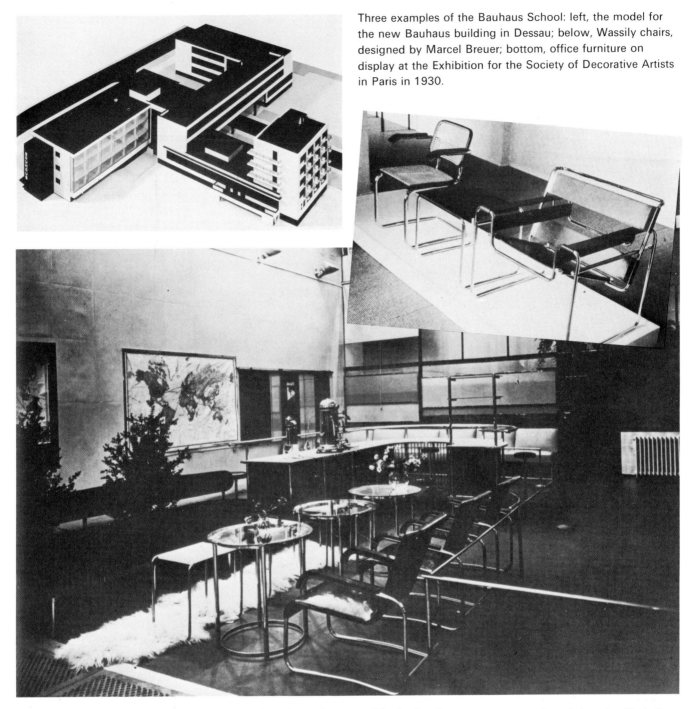

Three examples of the Bauhaus School: left, the model for the new Bauhaus building in Dessau; below, Wassily chairs, designed by Marcel Breuer; bottom, office furniture on display at the Exhibition for the Society of Decorative Artists in Paris in 1930.

He was impressed and excited by what he found, particularly with the possibilities demonstrated by architects like Philip Webb and Norman Shaw for creating a new style of domestic architecture which he felt could be synthesized into an entirely new concept of building when combined with the raw materials then being used in engineering—iron, steel, concrete and glass. Unlike William Morris—whose fiercely pure aesthetic sense admitted the need for 'decorative, noble, *popular* art' but denied it easy distribution—he also saw the potential of machine production. Morris had a romantically medieval concept of art, believing in 'dedicated craftsmen working directly with their materials.' He utterly rejected the values of the steam age, asserting that 'nothing of value' could be produced by machinery 'since mass production brought with it mass degradation. . . . Men living among such ugliness cannot conceive of beauty, and therefore cannot express it.'

Muthesius, however, was convinced that the disciplines of craftsmanship and industry could be combined and soon after his return to Germany announced the formation of the Deutscher Werkbund, set up in 1907, to improve standards in design and industry. The same year the architect, Peter Behrens, formerly head of the Düsseldorf School of Art, was appointed artistic consultant to the Allgemeine Elektrizitätgesellschaft (AEG) 'to design street lamps and other similar conveniences.' Behrens however began planning buildings—huge structures in steel and glass and concrete, for 'form,' he was fond of saying, 'follows function.' Surrounding him were a formidable collection of disciples including Le Corbusier, Hans Poelzig (who later designed the Grosses Schauspielhaus of Max Reinhardt), Bruno Taut, and Walter Gropius.

Gropius, however, left Behrens' studio in 1910 to set up his own practice. In 1911 the fruits of his master could be seen in the Fagus shoe-last factory at Alfeld-an-der-Leine, a transparent glass and steel structure with no supports at the corners—a revolutionary innovation which established him firmly in the front rank of the younger, more avant-garde architects.

After the First World War Walter Gropius, disillusioned but aflame with romantic yearnings, joined the *November-gruppe*, convinced that it was 'the accepted values in art and architecture and society which had led to the degradation of man's essential humanity.' 'After that violent inter-ruption,' he wrote, 'which kept me, like most of my fellow architects, from work for four years, every thinking man felt the necessity for an intellectual change of heart. Each in his own particular sphere of activity aspired to help in bridging the disastrous gulf between reality and idealism. It was then that the immensity of the mission of the archi-tects of my own generation first dawned on me. . . .'

In 1919 Gropius was given the opportunity to put his messianic ideas into practice. He was invited by the re-publican government to head an amalgamation of the two existing art schools in Weimar, the School of Arts and Crafts and the Academy of Fine Arts. He accepted and decided to call his new project 'Das Staatlich Bauhaus Weimar.'

Soon after taking up his appointment Gropius issued a proclamation, the cover of which was illustrated by a striking woodcut by Lyonel Feininger. 'The complete building,' it began, 'is the final aim of the visual arts. Their noblest function was once the decoration of buildings. Today they exist in isolation, from which they can be rescued only through the conscious co-operative effort of all craftsmen. . . . Architects, sculptors, painters we must all turn to the crafts. Art is not a "profession." There is an essential difference between the artist and the crafts-man. . . . Let us create a new guild of craftsmen, without the class distinctions which raise an arrogant barrier be-tween craftsman and artist. Together let us conceive and create the new building of the future, which will embrace architecture and sculpture and painting in one unity and which will rise one day toward heaven from the hands of a million workers like the crystal symbol of a new faith.'

This was a revolutionary concept indeed, and one which acted as a magnet to students from all over the country. In 1920 records show the Bauhaus supporting 221 students, made up of 200 Germans, fourteen Austrians, three Ger-mans from the Baltic countries, two Sudeten Germans and two Hungarians, on a comparatively slim budget of 206,206 marks ($50,000). As one student wrote '. . . I wonder what most Bauhaus members lived on. But the happiness and fullness of those years made us forget our poverty. Bauhaus members came from all social classes. They made a vivid appearance, some still in uniform, some barefoot, or in sandals, some with the long beards of artists or ascetics. Some came from the youth movements.'

They had a formidable collection of teachers, under whom they could learn typography, furniture design, rug making, pottery, bookbinding, how to work in glass, stone, wood and metal, and even dancing and stage management. Paul Klee delved into the intricacies of linear form, Wassily Kandinsky conducted his experiments with color, Lazlo Moholy-Nagy ran the preliminary course and was director of the metal workshops, Oscar Schlemmer was head of the department of fresco painting. Only an architectural work-shop was missing—Gropius kept his studio in Berlin, per-haps feeling that his disintegrating marriage to the com-poser Gustav Mahler's widow and the problems of raising funds for and administrating the Bauhaus were as much as he could cope with in Weimar itself.

For inevitably, despite the high ideals of teachers and students alike, there were those who opposed Gropius' central idea of uniting art and technology. Lyonel Feininger was one who felt that it was a 'misinterpretation' of art, as did the painter Johannes Itten, who eventually resigned from the Bauhaus in protest at the way things were going. But worse still were the difficulties which arose with the more conservative elements in the Weimar government who had become alarmed by the freethinking hydra it had helped to initiate and wanted to cut off a few of its more outrageous heads. In the end they threatened to get rid of Gropius and reduce the budget by half. At the eleventh hour, however, the Bauhaus was rescued from extinction by the Mayor of Dessau, who offered the school both a home and means of support in that small city, between Weimar and Berlin.

And there in the new building designed by Gropius himself and completed in 1926, the work went on. Marcel Breuer, who had come to the Bauhaus as an eighteen-year-old student in 1920, took charge of the furniture workshop where in 1925 he produced the first chair using tubular steel, followed three years later by his revolutionary canti-lever chair.

Away from Weimar or Dessau the Bauhaus also exerted a potent influence. In Berlin Mies van der Rohe (who, in fact, became the last director of the Bauhaus before it was closed by the Nazis in July 1933) conducted a perpetual love affair with glass—his project for an office building in the Friedrichstrasse entered in a competition in 1920 was a shimmering glass skyscraper, twenty storeys high, de-signed to let in 'the light of the sun, the moon and the stars.'

By comparison the buildings of the architect Eric Mendelsohn appeared awkward. Although, like Gropius and Mies van der Rohe, he had drawn inspiration from the *Novembergruppe* and shared its ideals, his work never had the pure uncluttered lines epitomized by Gropius' Dessau Bauhaus. Indeed his 'Einstein Tower' (a laboratory and observatory built for the scientist in the suburb of Potsdam was described by one writer as looking 'rather like an un-gainly spaceship' with 'its squat, concrete tower,' rising 'heavily from an elongated base.' Nevertheless Mendel-sohn was the busiest architect of his generation. He built suburban villas, department stores, and designed the head-quarters for the Metal Workers' Union, the Universum Movie Palace and the Columbus office buildings.

But, as Otto Friedrich pointed out, 'no one architect . . . not even a school of architecture can decisively affect a city that is already established.' For all their innovations and for all their talent and optimism there was not enough room in Berlin for the architects of the Twenties to fully realize their ideals. The allied bombs which destroyed Berlin achieved what neither they nor Albert Speer had been able to do, but it was at a price not even Hitler had been prepared to pay.

Above: Poster for the Charell Ballet at the New Operetta Theater. The composer was Friedrich Holländer who first gained a reputation by setting Kurt Tucholsky's poems to music. He eventually turned to the commercial theater and films and is best remembered for writing the music for Marlene Dietrich in *The Blue Angel*.
Left: The Communist slogan, 'Lenin shows them the way,' which was used during the elections until 1924.
Below: Advertisement for tea at Richard's Café.

An assortment of covers from two popular magazines in the 1920s, *Lustige Blätter* and *Der Junggeselle*.

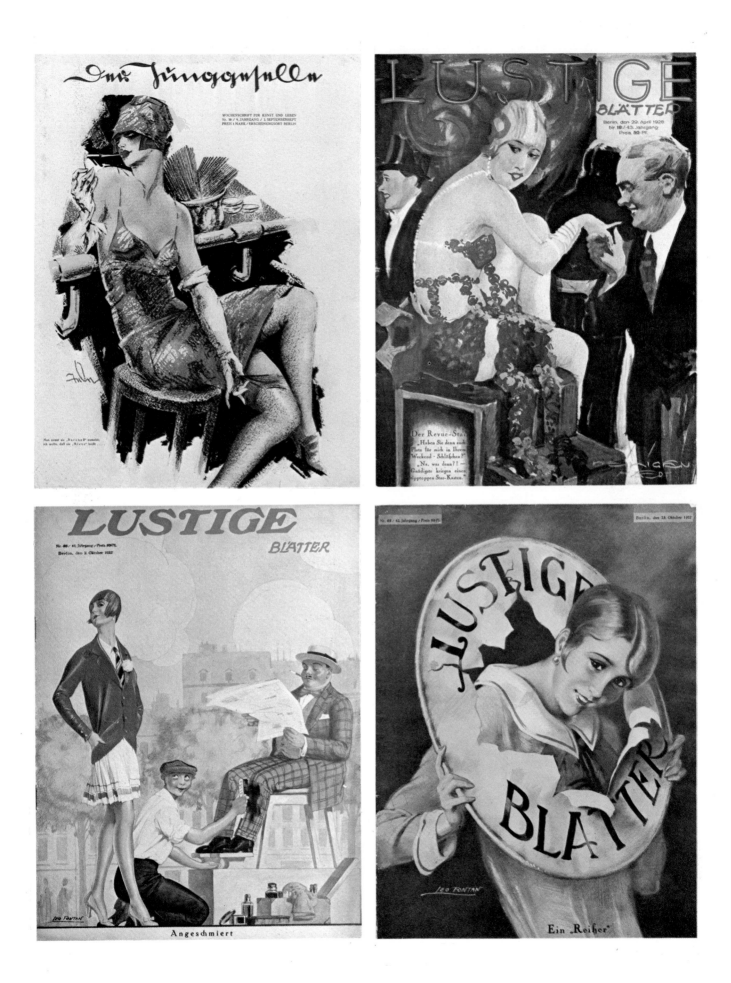

German painting reached its apogee during the 1919–33 period. Left: The Art Dealer Alfred Flechtheim, by Otto Dix. Above: Das Sternebild, by George Grosz. Above right: Untitled, by Grosz. Below: Beauty, I want to sing to You, by Grosz. Right: Comte St-Genois d'Anneaucourt, by Christian Schad.

Several cartoons from *Berliner Leben*, a popular magazine in the 1920s.

DIE WOCHE

Heft 40 Preis 50 Pf.
Berlin, 1. Okt. 1927

Die Woche did a special issue on Hindenburg in
October 1927. Right: A portrait of the President.
Above and below: Views of the Reichspresident's palace on
the Wilhelmstrasse.

Evelyn Dove and her troupe of cabaret artistes in 1930.

CABARET AND FILMSTADT

In 1945, just 26 days after the fall of Berlin, 33 young men climbed onto their bicycles and staged Berlin's first postwar bicycle race. Although they only managed a few laps, it was a symbolic gesture—a reminder of the glorious days between the wars when the huge Sports Palace in the Potsdamerstrasse (opened in 1910 to the strains of Richard Strauss conducting Beethoven's *Fifth Symphony*) was filled with the sound of cheering, as the crowd willed their heroes to perform feats of astounding endurance in the Six-Day Bicycle Race. Within a month of the surrender six theaters had opened, a cinema showed Hans Albers in *Grosse Freiheit Nr 7* (made under, but banned by, the Nazis) and Yehudi Menuhin returned to the city for an emotional concert with the Berlin Philharmonic conducted by Sergiu Celibadachi.

Berlin was still Berlin—it was still a city where anything could happen. But the spirit of 'Die Goldenen Zwanziger Jahre' (The Golden Twenties) had vanished—that elusive mood which produced such passionate participation in the novel and the bizarre, with Berliners rushing headlong to embrace everything from harnessing ostriches to flimsy carts, gambolling in the nude in earnest pursuit of 'Freikorperkultur' (Free Body Culture) to dancing until dawn through the 'light filled, sparkling, Champagne-bubbling, jazz droning, noisy . . . Berlin nights.'

Vaudeville shows, revues, literary cabarets, nightclubs, erotic Tanzbars were all packed with the pleasure-hungry. At the amusement palaces of the Wintergarten or the Scala, presided over by a master of ceremonies dressed in black and silver, 'maharajahs' lay on beds of nails and lively sketches were performed while the members of the audience ate hot dogs and drank cold beer. At the Metropol, the Admiralspalast and in Max Reinhardt's vast Grosses Schauspielhaus, which could seat nearly 5000 people, entertainment was provided which ranged from naked girls to the Tiller girls and from comics to Shakespeare, and in the Tanzbars anything could happen. 'Berlin,' Walter Nelson wrote, 'became notorious for its army of pimps, prostitutes, transvestites, fetichists and boy prostitutes, or Strichjungen.' Anita Berber danced nude on the stage of the White Mouse cabaret and 'used cocaine and morphine, was married and divorced, tried lesbian love and could be seen at every night club, boxing match, bicycle race, bar and party, usually leading an entourage of boxers, dancers, brawlers and barflies who helped her create a disturbance wherever she went.' Stefan Zweig also confirmed the decadence: 'All values were changed and . . . Berlin was transformed into the babylon of the world—bars, amusement parks, honky-tonks sprang up like mushrooms. . . . Along the entire Kurfürstendamm powdered and rouged young men sauntered . . . and in the dimly-lit bars one might see government officials and men of the world of finance tenderly courting drunken sailors without any shame. Even the Rome of Suetonius had never known such orgies as the balls of Berlin, where hundreds of men costumed as women and hundreds of women as men danced

Above: Germany's best professional dance team, Günther Mertins and Maud Stray, in 1930.

Far left: Society dancers step out to the tune of *My Man*, a song first made popular by the French singer, Mistinguett, and later by the American, Fanny Brice.
Left: Anni Cotti and Rudolf Dörry dance the Shimmy.
Above: Riccardo de Luca does the Charleston in 1926.

Left: A page boy on stilts astounds passers-by in a Berlin street.
Above: A businessman dictates to his secretary in a swimming pool when the summer heat went over 30°C in Berlin (86°F).
Below: The public swimming pool in Luna Park in 1924. It was notable because it tried to recreate a seaside atmosphere by simulating waves.
Right: Bride and groom leave a Berlin church for their honeymoon on a motorcycle.
Far right: A real Berliner enjoys his beer.
Below right: A hairdressing competition has two girls sporting the latest bob.

Above: The celebrated
writer, Erich Kästner, in 1925.
Right: The cabaret at the
White Mouse in the
Französischestrasse in 1925.

under the benevolent eyes of the police. In the collapse of all values a kind of madness gained hold, particularly in the bourgeois circles which until then had been unshakable in their probity.'

The collapse of all censorship, however, put an end to probity and led to an orgy of sexual experimentation. The Amusierkabarett flourished in a welter of smoke, drugs and transvestism, but more often than not they failed to live up to their promise of liberated fulfillment, proving disappointingly shabby and sadly naive. Erich Kästner captured the spirit of desperate permissiveness in his poem, 'Ragoût fin de siècle,' a verse of which ran:

Some here, from sheer wish to be perverted
Found they had to the norm reverted,
And if Dante had this place to visit
He's taken poison just to miss it.

And Christopher Isherwood, in *A Berlin Diary*, also described just such a bar—the Salome—which 'turned out to be very expensive and even more depressing than (he)

had imagined. A few stage lesbians and some young men with plucked eyebrows lounged at the bar, uttering occasional raucous guffaws or treble hoots, supposed, apparently, to represent the laughter of the damned. . . .'

The Eldorado on the Motzstrasse catered for the particularly dedicated transvestite; as one writer put it, there 'the arithmetic of love was not without its mistakes.' At the Residenzkasino the atmosphere was slightly less ambivalent but equally free and easy—each table was equipped with a telephone so that the customers could get to know each other without tedious preliminary formalities.

Cabaret, however, was not all naked girls and honky tonk. It had a serious side. Walter Mehring, editor of the magazine *Ulk*, was an explicitly political poet and writer of songs and lyrics who was a constant thorn in the flesh of the Weimar government, as Kurt Tucholsky whose biting aphorisms hit below the belt of left and right and whose songs were sung, according to Lisa Appignanesi, 'in all the best cabarets in Berlin.' These unrepentant critics and satirists castigated the war, inflation, General Ludendorff,

Above: The Winter Ball in 1933. One can see the return to more conventional fashions.

Above: The girls from the Mickey Mouse Revue.
Below: Chorus line from Berlin's Winter Garden, 1922.

the Freikorps, the oppression of workers, Weimar justice, the revolution and nationalism. Tucholsky in particular had a wide range of anti-nationalist jokes—for example: 'This continent is proud of itself and has a right to be. What they are proud of in Europe: Of being a German. Of being a Frenchman. Of being an Englishman. Of not being a German. Of not being an Englishman.'

The cabaret Schall und Rauch, started by Max Reinhardt before the war in the basement of his Grosses Schauspiel-haus, starred the singer and monologist Paul Graetz and the singer Gussy Holl, for whom Kurt Tucholsky wrote many songs and of whom he said 'Frankfurt has produced two great men . . . Goethe and Gussy Holl . . . she can do any-thing; hate and love, stroke and beat, sing and speak—there is no tone that is not part of her lyre.' And at the Cafe Grossenwahn was Rosa Valetti with her 'mobile features, flaming eyes and red hair' belting out her songs in a 'trum-petlike voice which could convey the horrors of the past war as well as the plight of the present.'

Above: Silk-stockinged Charleston addicts in 1926. The dance took Europe by storm in the 1920s.

Above: Nightclub artistes in 1926.
Right: Entertainment at a society party in 1925.
Bottom right: Willi Schäffers presents the cast from his revue *Pictures at an Exhibition*.
Bottom center: The audience and the stage of the Winter Garden.
Bottom far right: Scene from the revue of the Singer Midgets in 1928.

Below: Fritz Fischer and his Girls from the musical comedy *You Don't Need Any Money* in 1932.
Left: Scene from the 'Chinese' revue *Teeblüten* in 1927.
Below left: Naturism is satirized in the cabaret *Larifari* in 1929.
Bottom left: The Jackson Girls, a cabaret troupe, take a canoe ride on their day off.

PRIVATGELÄNDE DER
NACKTKULTURGEMEINDE
DES MITTELSTANDES E.V.

Right: Grock, the world's most famous clown, puts on his make-up.
Bottom: A juggling act at the Winter Garden.

Far left: These 'girls' were all men who frequented the transvestite bar Eldorado in the Motzstrasse.
Center left: Three couples left standing in the morning of the fourth day of a six-day dance marathon.
Left: Roulette in an illicit casino.
Below left: Street musicians dressed as Charlie Chaplin and 'the Kid,' Jackie Coogan.
Below: An unemployed man.

Knights and dancers in a children's revue produced in 1929 called *List of a Thousand Wishes* or as it was known in German, *Tausend Wunschzettel.*

Later, in 1929, after the National Socialist Germany Workers' Party had scored some success at the polls and brown shirts were seen everywhere in Berlin, Werner Finck, master of ceremonies at the Katacombe, kept up a perpetual barrage of insults at their expense, taking the inevitable comebacks in his stride. (To a brownshirt who shouted 'Dirty Jew' he replied, 'You're wrong—I only look this intelligent. . . .') His waspish tongue eventually needled the Nazis beyond endurance and the Katakombe was closed down in 1935. After a self-imposed exile Finck returned to Berlin after the war but found it a wanner, sadder place and without the monster of Nazism into which he could sink his sharp teeth, his bite declined. He died in 1978 without ever having regained his previous popularity.

Although the German Kabarett provided an outlet for political and cultural satire, it was by its very nature an intimate medium. The theater, on the other hand, provided entertainment on a far grander scale; indeed it was the opinion of many directors working in Berlin in the mid-1920s that it was not 'mere entertainment, not even just art, but an essential force in human life.' For it was within the theater and in drama that, as Frederick Ewen has pointed out, 'Germans found that outlet for their agitations, discontents and hopes that seemed denied them in real life. The theater, not the ballot-box or even political parties, represented the true arena of social activity for them.'

In the late nineteenth century two theatrical ventures were launched in Berlin. The first was the Freie Bühne, or Free Stage Movement, modelled on the Théâtre Libre in Paris, whose goal was theater free from all censorship and the need for commercial gain. The second was Die Freie Volksbühne, or The People's Stage, which aimed at bringing the theater to the working class, who, for a membership fee of fifty pfennig, were allotted tickets by lottery. The Free Stage Movement was directed by Otto Brahm, the son of a Hamburg merchant and the biographer of Schiller and

Below left: Trude Hesterberg, famous as an actress and as a cabaret director, in her dressing room.
Below: Hesterberg at home.
Right: Hanussen, a clairvoyant, in his 'laboratory.'
Far right: A revue dancer has her legs massaged.
Below right: Erwin Piscator, a photomontage by Sacha Stone.

Kleist. In 1889 Die Freie Bühne opened in typically controversial form with Ibsen's *Ghosts*, (a play already banned in Germany because of its references to syphilis).

But whereas the Free Stage Movement became an institution after Otto Brahm took over the directorship of the Deutscher Theater, the Volksbühne almost immediately ran into trouble. It had been discovered that the 'proletariat' maintained a healthy dislike of anything but the most conventional entertainment and resolutely refused to support the ideological and experimental productions staged for its benefit. As a result, the Volksbühne 'moved closer and closer to the bourgeois theater until, in 1913, they closed ranks.' Nevertheless the principle survived. 'Audience Associations' are still in existence in Berlin, members buying cheap season tickets and having them assigned by lottery when they come to the theater in the evening. Nowadays, however, the public are used to the vagaries of directors and take what comes, however avant-garde. Erwin Piscator, that enfant terrible of the Berlin theater who died in 1966, complained: 'The theater-going public is faithful and well-educated. People go to Shakespeare and Schiller and the newest incomprehensible Playwright of the Absurd. They sit straight in their seats, their hands held properly along the seams of their trousers, and never make a rude noise. What is my complaint? My complaint is that today's theater does not move these people. They come because it is the proper bourgeois thing to do. They do not come to be instructed, disturbed, or engaged. They are indifferent. We live in an age of indifference.'

But at the turn of the century, with Max Reinhardt taking over from Brahm at the Deutscher Theater, an electric current was running through the Berlin theater. Reinhardt, an actor who had performed in Brahm's company, was a theatrical magician, and as Gerhard Masur said, 'a wizard for whom the stage was not a moral, or an educational, and especially not a political institution,' but 'a magical contrivance with which to ravish and enthrall an audience.' Reinhardt was a colossus who straddled the Berlin theater for more than a decade. He was the Cecil B de Mille of the theater, a consummate showman whose innovative lighting and staging techniques were on the grand scale. 'He was,' as one writer commented, 'the master of gigantic productions and a genius of the mob scene.' His Grosses Schauspielhaus, first a market hall, then a circus arena, was converted into a huge theater—a dramatic dream translated into reality in 1919 by the architect Hans Poelzig, who turned it into a vast, fantastic, stalactite cave. It was not received with universal enthusiasm, and one observer felt that there was 'something quite frightening about it. It is a spiritual Luna Park in the shadow of the danse macabre.' Nevertheless the opening play, a characteristically magnificent production of Aeschylus' *Oresteia*, went down well with the critics—Fritz Engels of the *Berliner Tageblatt* calling it 'a real experience.'

As well as the Grosses Schauspielhaus, Max Reinhardt started the Kammerspiele, a small experimental theater in the Schumann Strasse above which was a school which he ran with his old associate Bertholt Held. There aspiring actors and actresses learned diction, elocution and Dalcroze eurythmics—in 1921 Marlene Dietrich, young and un-known and desperate for the sort of recognition only Reinhardt could give, asked to be allowed to give a reading. Bertholt Held heard her read from Hoffmannsthal's *Der Tod und der Tod* and was impressed, but her test-piece for Reinhardt (Gretchen's prayer to the Holy Virgin from *Faust*) left the great man 'cold and indifferent'—even though, as her biographer recalled, she 'cried real tears'—and she was turned away. Held, however, took pity on her and gave her private lessons. A year later she made her theatrical debut at the Kammerspiele in Somerset Maugham's *The Circle* and later appeared as the Widow with Elisabeth Bergner as Katharina in *The Taming of the Shrew* at the Grosses Schauspielhaus.

For all his legendary powers Reinhardt was not considered progressive enough by some of his younger contemporaries, many of whom believed drama to be not only an instrument for radical change, but also an effective means of revolution. It was not enough to see *Romeo and Juliet* at the Deutscher Theater actually in bed together; what was needed was a complete break with all bourgeois and capitalistic values and the establishment of a proletarian 'mass' theater.

The idea was not a new one, but in the disturbed climate of Berlin in the early Twenties it took on a new complexion. Visits from the Moscow theater under Constantin Stanislavski had been events in themselves, but even more intoxicating to progressive young directors were the ideas

Below: Max Reinhardt (1873–1943) at a rehearsal in the acting school he founded. He was the most famous producer of the Berlin theater at the time.

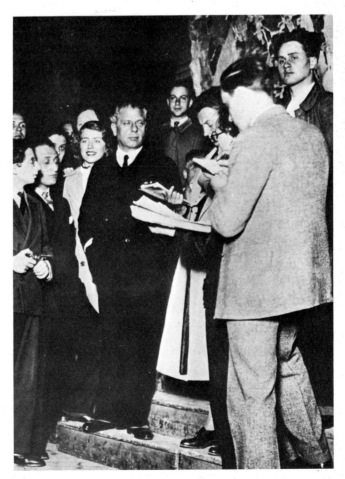

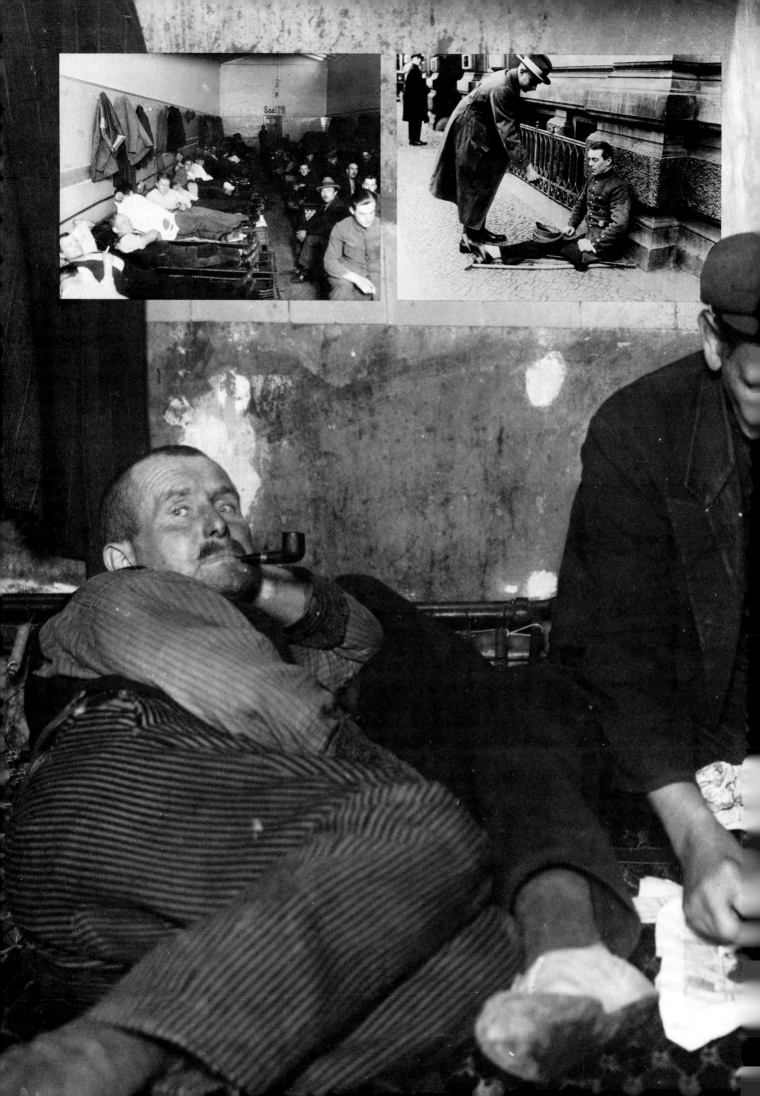

Far left: Men's dormitory in a doss house for the homeless in Berlin.
Center left: A wounded war veteran is reduced to begging.
Left: Poor children from the Wedding district get their school lunch, their only meal of the day.
Below: Men in a doss house share out their cigarettes and cigar butts which they found in the street.

being put forward by Stanislavski's associate, Vsevolod Meyerhold, who saw in the Russian revolution 'an unprecedented opportunity for the renewal of the theater.' He felt that the spectator should never forget for a minute that he was in the theater, and his 'constructivist' stage, which dispensed with curtains and made use of moveable sets, attempted to draw the audience into the performance as 'co-creators of the drama' by creating a 'symphony of motion.' Others went even further—the Russian Platon Kerzhenev advocated a proletarian 'mass' theater 'under the open sky' and Alexander Tairov 'utilized cubes, squares, pyramids, levels and inclines' and drew his inspiration from the Indian theater.

Invigorated by the flow of ideas from the Russian theater, various theatrical groups organized by the working class in Berlin attempted to spread the revolutionary message. This so-called 'agit-prop' movement, whose 'living newspapers' and 'mock-trials of the reactionary bourgeoisie' and unwieldly 'mass-pageants' involving up to 2000 'actors' and 50,000 spectators, provided an enthusiastic, if not always greatly talented, outlet for the participants. In Erwin Piscator, however, the dynamic young Bavarian actor who had directed a radical theater group in Königsberg until it went 'proudly bankrupt,' revolutionary Berlin at last found its theatrical catalyst, whose concept of a total theater had an effect so seismic that, as his disciple Bertolt Brecht wrote: 'The experiments of Piscator at once produced a thorough-going chaos in the theater. It did not aim only to provide a spectator with an experience, but wanted to wrest from him practical conclusions, make him take hold of life itself, and actively participate in living.' In 1919 Piscator founded the Proletarian Theater, announcing in its

first program: 'Comrades! The soul of the Revolution, the soul of the approaching society of the classless and communal culture represent our revolutionary feelings. The Proletarian Theater wishes to ignite this feeling and help keep it alive. The experiences awakened in us by socialist art fortify us in our consciousness of the seriousness and the greatness of the historical mission of our class.' Undeterred by the primitive conditions Piscator, ignoring the conventional theater, took his small band of untrained and previously unemployed actors into the slums and beerhalls of Berlin.

Below: *Casanova* staged at the Grosses Schauspielhaus.
Right: Claire Waldoff and Lamberts Paulsen.
Below right: Program for *Hoppla wir leben*, a left-wing revue directed by Erwin Piscator.

Sonnabend, den 3. September, abends 7 Uhr
URAUFFÜHRUNG

HOPPLA — WIR LEBEN!

Ein Stück
von ERNST TOLLER
Inszenierung: Erwin Piscator
Musik: Edmund Meisel Bühnenbild: Traugott Müller
Film: Curt Oertel
Chansontext: Walter Mehring

Personen

Karl Thomas	Alexander Granach
Eva Berg	Sybille Binder
Wilhelm Kilman	Oscar Sima
Albert Kroll	Ernst Busch
Frau Meller	René Stobrawa
Ein Gefangener	Leopold Lindtberg
Aufseher Rand	Karl Hannemann
Leutnant Baron Friedrich	Werner Kepich
Prof. Lüdin	Leonhard Steckel
Wärter	Adolf Fischer
Graf Lande	Werner Hollmann
Fritz	Heinrich Oberländer
Grete	Bertl Eisenberg
Kriegsminister	Paul Pruegel
Bankier	Eugen Jensen
Sein Sohn	Hans Maria Böhmer
Pickel	Paul Graetz
Frau Kilman	Margarete Wellhoener
Lotte Kilman	Lilo Dammert
Diener im Ministerium	Gerhard Bienert
1. Arbeiter	Leopold Lindtberg
2. Arbeiter	Heinz Greif
3. Arbeiter	Gerhard Bienert
Wirt	Konrad Niedt
Wahlleiter	Ludwig Roth
Wahlbeisitzer	Erich Stollhoff
1. Stimmzettelverteiler	Adolf Fischer
2. Stimmzettelverteiler	Rolf Gärtner
3. Stimmzettelverteiler	Hermann Gerber
Alte Frau	Lotte Löbinger
Oberkellner	Paul Herm
Hausdiener	Albert Venohr
Telegraphist	Kurt Weiße
Pikkolo	Alfred Schäfer
Leutnant Frank	Heinz Greif
1. Polizist	Hermann Gerber
2. Polizist	Gerhard Bienert
Polizeioberst	Paul Herm
Sekretärin	Eva Gottgetreu

Chanson-Vortrag: Kate Kühl
Damen, Herren, Volk.
Pause nach dem 5. Bild (Wahlbild)

Klavier und Viertelton-Harmonium werden von der
Firma August Förster, Löbau i. Sachsen und Berlin, gestellt.

If ever he had wanted concrete proof of his view that the theater was 'a parliament and the audience a legislative body' he had it on 15 January 1920, when he staged a play called *The Cripple* in the working-class district of Neukölln. The scenery, designed by John Heartfield, was not ready for the opening night, and Piscator was obliged to go ahead 'with nothing but a black curtain, a bare stage and a few props.' At the beginning of the second act Heartfield appeared with his scenery. After a heated argument during which director and scenic designer both blamed each other for the state of affairs, Piscator turned to the audience and asked them what they would like. An 'overwhelming majority' decided in favor of the scenery being installed, despite the inevitable interruption in the performance. 'We had suddenly broken with the old course of theatre,' Piscator recorded. 'Audience and stage were united in one desire.'

Piscator found, however, like the originators of Die Freie Volksbühne before him, that the ideals of the proletarian theater sooner or later came up against the unfortunate desire of the average worker to escape from his drab environment after dark into a world of light, color and fantasy rather than into one of bleak realism. He wanted circuses, operettas, revues and girls, not revolutionary tracts. Piscator flirted briefly with the Volksbühne when he attempted to stage a realistic account of the Berlin revolution, a gigantic production 'consisting' as Frederick Ewen wrote, 'of what Piscator called a "Praktikabel"—terraces, inclines, stairways, platforms on revolving planes. Everything was there: speeches, essays, newspaper reports, addresses, flyers, photos, films of war and revolution, historical personalities ...,' followed by a play called *Storm over Gottland*, a pro-Bolshevik account of the Russian revolution, thinly disguised as a drama of the Hanseatic period, ended in failure.

Commercial success came after the rich husband of the film actress, Tilla Durieux, offered to set Piscator up in bourgeois splendor in the Theater am Nollendorfplatz. Here between 1927 and 1930 he was able to synthesize all his ideas, gathering round him a team of writers which included George Grosz and Bertolt Brecht and actors such as Tilla Durieux, Helene Weigel, Paul Graetz, Ernst Deutsch, Ernst Busch, Alexander Granach and Max Pallenberg. The first play staged by Piscator at the Nollendorfplatz was Ernst Toller's *Hoppla wir leben*, a stirring drama dealing with the reality or otherwise of insanity.

In this Hotel on earth,
the creme of society is our guest.
They take things easy,
devoid of the burdens of life.
The enemies have been thrashed.
Give the cripple there a dime!

We ourselves run short.
The ministers, thinkers and poets—
they are the same faces time and again.
It's all like it has been before the war
and like before the next—
with Charleston we have battle music.

Hoppla, we are living!
And when do we square accounts with them!

Above: Carola Neher and Hermann Thimig, members of second cast for *The Threepenny Opera* in the Theater am Schiffbauerdamm in 1928.
Far left: Scene from the opening of *The Threepenny Opera* in 1928.
Above left: Scene from the second act of Bert Brecht's *Drums in the Night* in 1922.
Left: Harald Paulsen as Macheath, Roma Bahn as Polly and Erich Ponto as the Beggar King in the first production of *The Threepenny Opera* in 1928.
Below left: Another scene from the Brecht-Weill play.
Below: Bert Brecht.

Left: Lilian Harvey and Willy Fritsch were two of UFA's
greatest singing stars in the 1930s.
Right: Fritz Lang, the renowned film director, on the set of
Woman on the Moon in 1928.

This was closely followed by Alexei Tolstoy's *Rasputin*, a
controversial production which provoked law suits involving the exiled Kaiser Wilhelm and a Russian financier.
For another production, Jaroslav Hašek's *The Good Soldier
Schweik*, Piscator had a double treadmill stage with pro-
jections and a cartoon film by George Grosz.

Bertolt Brecht, who also worked closely with Piscator on
The Good Soldier Schweik, had come to Berlin in 1924 from
Munich where his *Trommeln in der Nacht* (*Drums in the
Night*) had already been performed, and where, a month
after he arrived in Berlin, his *Life of Edward II of England*
was also produced. A critic of the Berliner Börsen-Courier
wrote of him at that time: '. . . the name Bert Brecht will
be remembered for reasons other than attractive alltera-
tion . . . he has a wild, prizeworthy, young talent, as long
as one does not demand that a twenty-year-old begin at his
peak. . . .'

Although deeply influenced by Piscator of whom he
wrote, 'For Piscator theater was a parliament and the
audience a legislative body. Before this body were visibly
set the great public questions that demanded decisions.'
Brecht himself took a more pragmatic view. Despite his
flirtation with Marxism and his persistent reading of the
'classics' (Engels, Lenin and Marx), he came to the con-
clusion that without audience appeal even Total Theater
had no value—although he did not give up the idea of the
theater as a means of educating the masses. 'Today's stage,'
he wrote, 'is completely makeshift. To view it as having to
do with the intellect, with art, is a misapprehension. Theater
deals with a vaguely comprehended public . . . the despair-
ing hope of the theater is to keep a hold on its public by
constantly capitulating to its taste. But unless the public is
seen in terms of the class struggle it must be rejected as the
source of a new style.'

The boxing ring exerted a strong fascination over Brecht
(as it did over Shaw and Hemingway). For there, he said,
in marked contrast to the conventional theater, the public
'knows exactly why they buy tickets of admission . . . and
what is being offered to them. They get fun, sport, ease.'
They also got a sense of physical excitement and the freedom
to wander around and to smoke if they so desired—another
Brechtian hobby-horse: 'One lone cigar-smoking individual at a performance of Shakespeare,' he wrote, 'would
bring about the downfall of all of western art. I would
gladly see a public smoking at a performance—particularly
for the sake of the actors. It would be impossible, I believe,
for an actor to perform in an unnatural, convulsive, and
antiquated manner in the presence of a smoker in the pit.'

Brecht's biggest popular success came in 1928 with his
singspiel, inspired by John Gay's *Beggar's Opera* of 1728,

Above right: Composer Oskar Strauss, film director Ernst
Lubitsch and American film comedian Harold Lloyd at
Berlin's airport. Lubitsch left for Hollywood in 1922 and
made successful satirical films.
Right: The French *chanteuse*, Mistinguett, visits Berlin.

Far left: Unemployed wait for soup at a Berlin doss house in December 1930.

Left: One of Germany's millions of unemployed sleeps with his worldly belongings on the Potsdam Bridge in 1930.

Below: A women's doss house in Berlin in 1930. After the apparent recovery of the German economy in 1924–29, economic and political stability collapsed in 1930.

Above: Pola Negri and Emil Jannings, two of Germany's greatest film stars, in *Vendetta*. They starred together in many of Lubitsch's films.

Above: Pola Negri as a nurse in *Vendetta*. She went to Hollywood where she repeated her success but Jannings never mastered English and returned.

Die Dreigroschenoper (*The Threepenny Opera*), which had words by Brecht and music by the composer Kurt Weill. The plot, which concerned the love of a girl (Polly Peachum) for a highwayman (MacHeath), her father's disapproval and revenge, MacHeath's path of seduction and eventual betrayal at the hands of a prostitute (Jenny Diver), and his dramatic reprieve on the brink of the Gallows, was an ideal vehicle for Brecht's Epic Theater. As Otto Friedrich pointed out in his book *Before the Deluge*, although Brecht was determined to turn the *Beggar's Opera* into an illustration of class conflict, 'he could not resist the temptation to strengthen Gay's rather stilted work with his own sense of drama.' This was not, after all, surprising. Brecht was both a playwright and a poet with the dramatist's nose for a telling pause or an ironic twist to a plot and the poet's sense of rhythm, and it was his recognition of unerring sense of drama that brought the audience at the Theater am Schiff-bauerdamm to their feet in wild enthusiasm at the first night on 31 August 1928. The production made overnight stars of many of the cast, notably Lotte Lenya, Kurt Weill's wife, who took the part of Jenny Diver, and it made both Brecht and Weill rich men.

The critics were divided. One called it a breakthrough into a 'world where the line between tragedy and humor has vanished'; others were less flattering: the *Krauz-Zeitung* referring disparagingly to 'literary necrophilia.' The influential critic Alfred Kerr of the *Berliner Tageblatt* was initially enthusiastic, calling the performance 'a magnificent evening,' but when the *Songs of the Dreigroschenoper* were published in 1929 he denounced Brecht for plagiarism. He claimed that some of the songs bore a more than passing resemblance to the poetry of François Villon in their German translation by K L Ammer.

Needless to say Brecht dismissed these charges with characteristically contemptuous references to bourgeois notions of 'property,' but he was not immune to the jibes of his contemporaries, Kurt Tucholsky being particularly caustic: 'Who wrote that piece/It's by Bertolt Brecht/Well, who wrote that piece?'

A few years later in 1931 the Austrian director Georg Wilhelm Pabst turned *The Threepenny Opera* into a film, which, according to Siegfried Kracauer, was 'less adequate than the stage production of 1928.' Brecht himself was so disappointed with the result which he felt had distorted a fundamental part of his message, that he sued the producers. 'I kept trying to see what was going on in the studio,' he wrote, 'Not even once did they let me see the final script. From a third party I learned that the script had two additional authors. They barred me from the studio. Since no one consulted me about the style of *The Threepenny Opera*, the public will find something totally different than it expected.'

It was a complaint which became familiar to many successful authors. (Hemingway disapproved of the film made from *A Farewell to Arms* and Christopher Isherwood was said to have been dissatisfied with *Cabaret*). But Brecht could have been forgiven for expecting better of Pabst, a socially conscious director—who had come into films via the theater, for which he felt there was no artistic future—and who was much influenced by the spirit of 'Neue Sachlichkeit' (New Objectivity) which pervaded the cinema after 1924. This expression was coined by the director of the Mannheim Museum, Gustav Hartlaub, to describe the new realism in painting, a movement he said, which was 'related to the general contemporary feeling in Germany of resignation and cynicism after a period of exuberant hopes (which had previously found an outlet in expressionism).'

After 1924, as Siegfried Kracauer has pointed out, the German cinema underwent a significant change. The 'revolution' had fizzled away, inflation was stilled, but the return to comparative social stability on such terms was accompanied for many by an inescapable sense of loss. The moment for radical change had come, the victory of the proletariat had been in sight, but it had slipped away in a welter of confusion, bankruptcy, hunger and unemployment. Disillusion was the touchstone of the new realism and in the cinema it reflected the need of film-makers to represent the world as it really was rather than to explore the outer fringes of human experience.

Below: The UFA lot at Neubabelsberg, the largest film studio in Europe between the wars.

Above: Max Schmeling, the heavyweight boxer turned actor, in a scene from *Love in the Ring*.

Such dark fantasies as those which swirled around the expressionistic and fatalistic film, *The Cabinet of Dr Caligari*, written by Hans Janowitz and Carl Mayer and directed by Robert Wiene in 1920, gave way to a more straightforward approach, epitomized by Pabst's film, *Secrets of a Soul* (1926) which probed the secrets of the mind in a wholly prosaic way—through the analyst's couch. In *The Cabinet of Dr Caligari* the relationship between the mysterious Dr Caligari and his 'tool,' the somnambulist Cesare explores the persuasive, tyrannical powers of hypnotism and delves into the inner reaches of the soul. Dr Caligari unlocked a Pandora's box of oppression and mad-

Above: The great actress Elizabeth Bergner in the film *Miss Else*, which was based on an Arthur Schnitzler novel.
Right: Bergner on stage in *Saint Joan* by Shaw in 1925.
She went to England in 1933.
Opposite right: Bergner in *Miss Else*. She was considered to be one of the greatest dramatic actresses of that time.

ness and he was left in a state of chaos, suffering the delusions of the insane. In *Secrets of the Soul*, a professor of chemistry (played by Werner Krauss) was subject to disturbing dreams, but regular sessions with an understanding and competent psychiatrist soon freed him from his inconvenient inhibitions, and he returned to the 'sane' world a happy man.

The Cabinet of Dr Caligari was one of the first films to profit from the 'shock of freedom' of the postwar cinema. For although the German cinema had begun in 1895, (two months before the Lumière brothers in Paris) with Max and Emil Skladanowsky showing their 'bioscop' in the Berlin Wintergarten, the attitude of prewar film directors to the new medium had remained one of cautious experimentation rather than confident expansion.

Until 1910 Germany had no film industry of her own and, even after two film studios were built at Tempelhof and Neubabelsberg, the Berlin public were still flocking to foreign films—Italian, Danish, and, especially popular, the American Western. Homegrown films were at that time too esoteric for mass audiences, and directors had not yet rid themselves of the habit of transferring stage techniques lock, stock and barrel to the screen, rather than approaching the medium in a completely fresh way. (An example was

Max Reinhardt's pantomime *Summurun*, made into a film in 1910, which apparently 'bored its audience by wasting 2000 meters on an exact duplication of the original stage performance.')

The outbreak of the First World War abruptly removed all foreign competition from the German film industry. Faced with the prospect of filling the gap, German film-makers rose instantly to the challenge, and the studios at Tempelhof and Neubabelsberg turned out scores of patriotic dramas (to send to the front) as well as melodramas, farces and comedies. The number of film companies increased between 1913 and 1919 from 28 to 245. In 1917 General Ludendorff, seeing the cinema's obvious propaganda potential, ordered the merging of the principle film companies into one concern—the powerful monopoly, UFA (Universum Film AG). After the 'revolution,' however, the Social Democrats renounced the government's one-third interest in the film industry, and as Otto Friedrich put it, 'abolished all censorship and turned the movie-makers loose to produce whatever the public wanted.'

It was in this atmosphere of challenge and freedom that *The Cabinet of Dr Caligari* was born. But there were other less rarified films being produced for the delectation of a by now insatiable public, prepared not only to queue for the privilege of seeing them but also willing to pay up to five marks for a ticket. (One Berliner wrote rather sourly, 'For that much I could have attended *Parsifal*!') A performance of *Parsifal*, however, for all its undoubted attractions, did not generate the same excitement as sitting in a darkened room watching Pola Negri play *Carmen*.

Carmen was directed by a young actor turned film director, who had initially worked with Max Reinhardt on the stage and then himself directed a series of slapstick comedies during the war—the legendary Ernst Lubitsch. The relationship between Lubitsch and his leading lady, the Polish actress Pola Negri, an equally strong-minded and idiosyncratic star and the daughter of a gypsy violinist, was a stormy one. She herself persuaded him to give her her first big screen part—in *Vendetta*—and he used her again with striking success in *Die Augen der Mumie Ma* (*The Eyes of the Mummy*), an 'Egyptian-exotic' drama concerning an Egyptian religious fanatic (played by Lubitsch's friend, Emil Jannings) who pursued a woman (Pola Negri) and eventually destroyed her.

Pola Negri was suggested for the role of *Carmen* (which was shown in America as *Gypsy Blood*) by the film promoter Paul Davidson, who approached Lubitsch saying, 'What a role for Negri'—reminding him of 'her raven hair, flashing

eyes, and seductive smile that could turn a saint from his vows.' Lubitsch, however, was unreceptive: 'Are you starting up with that temperamental Polish witch again? Nee, Nee, ausgeschlossen—that's not for Papa Simon's son!' Nevertheless Davidson and Pola Negri got their way, and Lubitsch did not live to regret it; it was his first international screen hit, and it established Pola Negri as 'Germany's foremost screen actress.'

Others followed—the comedy *Oyster Princess* with Ossi Oswalda, 'the Mary Pickford of Germany' in the title role and in 1919 the epic *Madame du Barry* with Emil Jannings as Louis XV and Pola Negri as the milliner's apprentice who became the king's mistress. This ran for three months in Berlin's biggest cinema, the UFA Palast-am-Zoo. Encouraged by its phenomenal success, Lubitsch repeated the formula with *Anna Boleyn* and *The Loves of Pharaoh*, both of which were planned on a grand scale and used hitherto undreamed numbers of extras (over 2000 apiece) to create scenes of unparalleled splendor and magnificence.

The public did not only queue for romantic epics however. There was a seamier side to the film industry, which the relaxation of censorship in 1918 did nothing to deter. Films with titles such as *Lost Daughters*, *Different from Others* and *A Man's Girlhood* proliferated, sometimes

Left: Emil Jannings in 1930, the year he played Professor Unrat in *The Blue Angel*.
Below: Audition time for the Fräulein number at the Scala in 1934.

Above: Heinz Rühmann, Adolf Wohlbrück, Renate Müller and Jenny Jugo in *Allotria*. Wohlbrück went to England and changed his name to Anton Wallbrook.

masquerading under the guise of 'sex education,' as in *Wege zur Kraft und Schönheit* (*Roads to Strength and Beauty*) made in 1925. There were, as one writer said, 'as many hard-core porno films in the Berlin of the Twenties as you could find half a century later on New York's Forty-Second Street.'

'Mountain' films also had a strong following—*Die Weisse Holle von Pitz Palu* (*The White Hell of Pitz Palu*), starring Luis Trenker and Leni Riefenstahl and made in 1929, was the most successful, but there were others, such as *Ski Wunder* (*The Wonder of Skis*, 1920), *Der Kampf um den Berg* (*Struggle with the Mountain*, 1921) and *Der Heilige Berg* (*The Holy Mountain*, 1926). As Luis Trenker said: 'Mountain climbing demands unparalleled performances . . . it is not the broad path of the masses but the narrow track of those who have selectively and systematically strengthened their talents, of those who know the technical aspects of climbing, those who have grown to conquer the mountain.' It had an irresistible appeal to the mystical sense of nationalism buried deep in every German heart, longings which Leni Riefenstahl was to exploit some years later in her masterpiece *Triumph des Willens*.

In 1930 the film critic Harry A Potakin wrote in an issue of *Cinema*: '. . . Germany is approaching a political crisis, and with it an intellectual and aesthetic crisis . . .'—an observation which few by then would have denied. The crash of the Wall Street stock market on 24 October 1929 had effectively amputated the American loans which had been the lifeblood of the German economy for the past five years, throwing an intolerable strain on the financial structure of the country, and the slump in world trade led to a dramatic loss of exports. Millions were unemployed, thousands of businesses collapsed, and in July 1931 the Darmstädter und Nationalbank failed, forcing the government in Berlin temporarily to close down all banks. And when the election returns came in on 14 September 1930,

Right: Listening to an oversized loudspeaker in the Kaiserdamm.

Right: Tempelhof airfield in Berlin in 1928.
Center right: The café at Tempelhof in 1929.
Far right: Passengers show their tickets after they disembark at Tempelhof.
Below: The commercial airport at Tempelhof.

LUFT HANSA
SCHÖNBURG

they revealed a gain of over five million votes for the Nazi party, giving them 107 seats in the Reichstag and making them the second largest party in Parliament. 'Never in my life,' wrote their leader, Adolf Hitler, in the Nazi press, 'have I been so well disposed and inwardly contented as in these days. For hard reality has opened the eyes of millions of Germans to the unprecedented swindles, lies and betrayals of the Marxist deceivers of the people.'

Allegory is a notoriously evocative medium of expression—by its very nature it uses one set of actions to imply another suggestively similar one. And if ever there was a film which transmitted, through its images of attraction and submission, corruption and sadism, self-pity and despair, the confusion of the German psyche at that time, it was *Der Blaue Engel* (*The Blue Angel*). It was, Siegfried Kracauer said, 'as if the film implied a warning, for those screen figures anticipate what will happen in real life a few years later. The boys are born Hitler youths. . . .'

The Blue Angel, first shown in 1930, was based on *Professor Unrat*, the novel by Heinrich Mann, a macabre tale which 'stigmatized the peculiar vices of German Bourgeois society.' It was adapted for the screen by Carl Zuckmayer, and Eric Pommer of UFA invited the Hollywood director, Joseph von Sternberg, to Berlin to direct the film, and Emil Jannings was cast in the role of the middle-aged professor who is seduced by a cabaret singer.

The part of the singer, Lola-Lola, proved more difficult to fill. Dozens of hopeful young beauties came to the studios for auditions, but none possessed the essential, if elusive, quality for which von Sternberg was searching. Carl Zuckmayer, who had seen the actress Marlene Dietrich in the satirical revue *Zwei Kravatten* (*Two Neckties*) at the Berliner Theater, wanted her for the part, but Eric Pommer was said to have screamed 'Not that whore' and refused to contemplate it. Von Sternberg, however, went to the Berliner Theater to see for himself. 'He knew at once,' wrote Charles Higham, Marlene Dietrich's biographer, 'that he had his Lola-Lola. The role of Mabel was the essence of Berlin, sexual and cynical . . . satiated with wordly pleasures. But there was another quality as well: a quality of tenderness and warmth, a womanliness alongside the veiled masculinity of the direct stare. This quality of sex without gender proved intoxicating to the young director.'

For Emil Jannings, however, it was a dispiriting experience. Already a major star, he found his prestige evaporating in the face of such dynamic competition. When the composer Friedrich Holländer finished 'Falling in Love Again,' Jannings said crossly to his co-star: 'If you sing that, my girl, I'll be finished! Nobody will ever see *me* on the screen!' So embittered did he become that when, during one scene he was obliged to pretend to strangle her, he flung himself on her with such genuine fury that he had to be prised loose—an episode which very nearly led to his prosecution for attempted murder.

Right: The actor, Alexander Moissi, in *The Other Side* before his death in 1925.
Opposite top: Lilian Harvey, the English actress who made her career in Germany, arrives at Tempelhof.
Opposite bottom: Harvey in the UFA silent film *Keusche Susanne* in 1926.

Despite Jannings' forebodings, the role of the humiliated Professor immortalized him and showed him to be, in the opinion of one critic, 'one of the greatest actors in cinema history.' And as for Marlene Dietrich, the first night of *The Blue Angel* was a triumph that has passed into legend. Her langorously impassive, insolent, portrayal of the callous Berlin prostitute, with her husky voice and her long legs, brought the audience to its feet shouting her name over and over again. It was not, however, only the hypnotic powers of Marlene Dietrich which turned *The Blue Angel* into an international hit. Its underlying theme was sadism, and if, as Siegfried Kracauer has asserted, *The Blue Angel* was an 'important statement on the psychological situation of the time' then, hindsight or not, it boded ill for the German people.

A propaganda float passes through Berlin's streets campaigning for President von Hindenburg's re-election in 1932

MUSIKSTADT

On 12 April 1929, when he was twelve years old, the violinist Yehudi Menuhin made his debut as a soloist in Berlin. Although he had already performed in other cities—in San Francisco (at the age of ten), Paris and New York—it was the Berlin concert which was held to be crucial for his adult career, for, as Menuhin wrote in his autobiography, 'Berlin was then the musical capital of the "civilized" world, its prestige founded on the music of the past and flourishing still in great orchestra and conductors, not to mention the most informed audiences to be found anywhere.' To be acclaimed in Berlin was to achieve world fame, and without its seal of approval no aspiring soloist, and particularly an American, could hope for more than a tepid response in his own country; in America the musical world was dominated by German conductors and a concert in Berlin and Dresden carried full-length reviews in American newspapers.

In consequence it was a nerve-wracking ordeal, even for a child prodigy with Yehudi Menuhin's startling gifts. The program chosen was ambitious—three concerti by Bach, Beethoven and Brahms, and, if this were not enough, on the morning of the concert there was a three-hour public rehearsal ('almost as important as the concert itself') followed by a gargantuan lunch given in his honor by the all-powerful agent, Louisa Wolff.

Despite the rigorous pre-concert program—one from

Below: Albert Einstein was forced to leave Germany in the early 1930s.

which most current performers would recoil in horror—the performance itself was an unqualified success. Even Menuhin, a modest man, had to admit when recording the episode that the response had been 'enthusiastic.' Indeed, he added, 'The Philharmonie's (sic) management, fearing the enthusiasm was getting out of hand, went to the lengths of summoning the police to restore order.' The scientist Albert Einstein, himself a keen, if erratic, violinist, was so overcome that he came backstage crying, 'Now I know there is a God in Heaven.'

Not all soloists had such happy experiences. In 1890 the flamboyant Polish pianist, Ignace Jan Paderewski, was engaged to give a concert with the Berlin Philharmonic, conducted at that time by Hans von Bülow, the first item of which was to be his own piano concerto. To his surprise and chagrin, however, he found von Bülow in an inexplicably irritable frame of mind and the orchestral playing mediocre to the point of incompetence. Paderewski, ever sensitive to the slightest insult, was mortified, suspecting a plot to put him at a disadvantage. Outraged, he recorded the incident in his memoirs:

'How I went through that concerto I really do not understand to this day, because there were so many mistakes, so

Below: Arnold Schönberg, the great composer.
Right: Author Dr Alfred Döblin during the filming of his social-critical novel *Berlin-Alexanderplatz*.
Below right: Erich Kleiber (center), director of the Berlin Philharmonic, at the Zoo railway station.

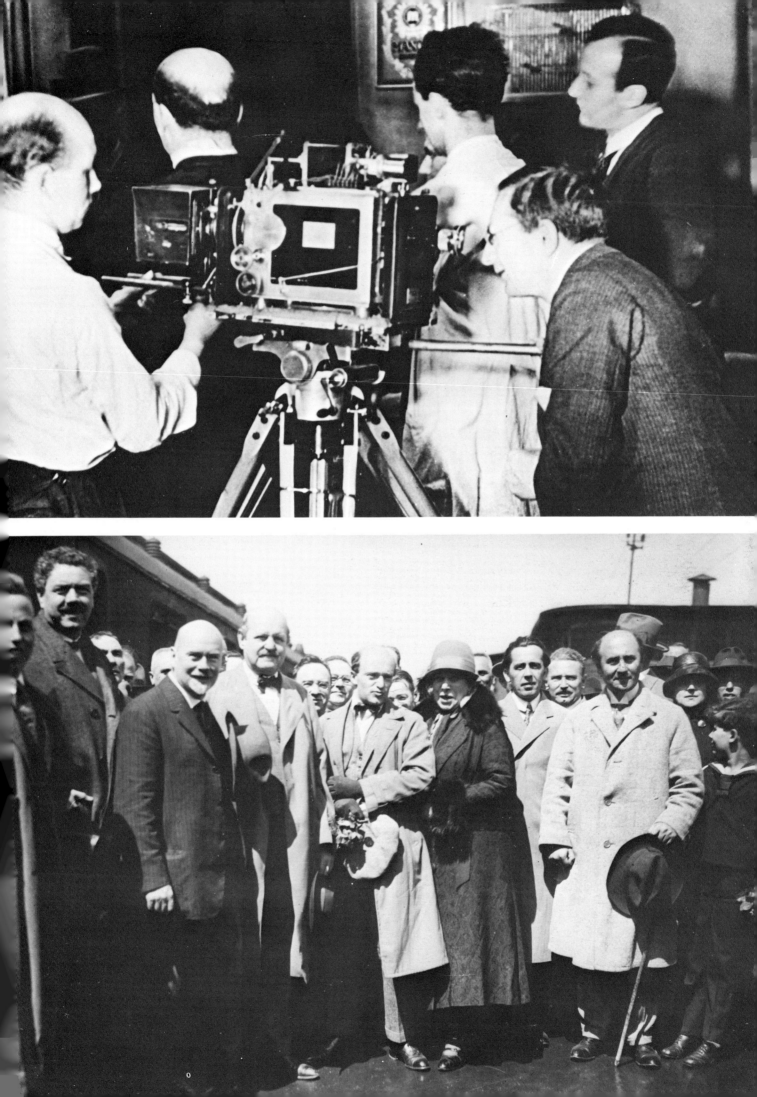

Above: Alfred Döblin at his medical practice in the Schönhauser Allee. Döblin wrote about Germany's collective experience and the human condition.
Right: Two of the *Chocolate Kiddies*, a jazz revue which caused a sensation in Berlin.

many errors on the part of the orchestra and the conductor, von Bülow. It was frightful! It was a nightmare! The whole performance was an agony! . . . It was a massacre!' There was, however, worse to come. During the playing of some solos in the second half of the program, the unpredictable von Bülow, 'who had elected to sit beside the piano that day, suddenly jumped up, pushed his chair back, and ran quickly off the stage and disappeared. . . . People began to whisper and everyone became very restless and uneasy. . . . Von Bülow had completely destroyed the mood.'

Not surprisingly, the critics were unsympathetic. 'Why,' wrote one journal, 'does this Pole come here? What does he want from an audience like our Philharmonic Society? He has no place with us. Because he wrote that little Minuet does he think he can impose upon us that tedious, abominable, dull concerto of his? How ridiculous!' Luckily for Paderewski, he was not a man to be destroyed by such a reception, even though the critics remained uniformly hostile after other concerts in Berlin (even if the audience, especially the women, had fallen under his spell). He had a perfectly good remedy. He would never return to Berlin. 'I shall never go back,' he said in 1933. 'Never. I shall never play in Berlin again. And I have never done so . . . even up to three years ago; I still had offers from Berlin, invitations from the Government even, to play, with the assurance that I would be received with all the acclaim and honors due to me not only as an artist but as a statesman. I have always declined, and I am not sorry for it.'

Another flamboyant figure who had rather more success

in Berlin was the Italian pianist and composer, Ferruccio Busoni, who came to the city in 1894 and who in 1920 was appointed teacher of a master class in composition at the Prussian Academy of Arts on the strength of his massive Concerto for piano and Male Chorus, and his operas *Arlecchino* and *Doktor Faust*. Although handicapped by narrow hands, he was a charismatic concert performer. One writer recorded the program for a 'typical recital' as being 'Beethoven's *Hammarklavier Sonata*, plus all four Chopin Ballades and the *A-flat Polonaise*, ending with Liszt's incredibly difficult *Reminiscences de Robert le Diable*.' His contemporary, Arthur Schnabel, the great interpreter of Beethoven's piano music, called Busoni 'the greatest figure —there is nobody like him.' Busoni reciprocated—but not until Schnabel was forty. Then, he told him, 'Schnabel, you are acquiring a face.' It was the highest compliment Busoni could pay.

By the nature of things Berlin attracted an extraordinary collection of musicians. Pianists like Claudio Arrau, Wilhelm Backhaus (another Beethoven specialist), Rudolph Serkin and the legendary Vladimir Horowitz—whose Garboesque flirtations with his public have made him possibly the most expensively promoted pianist of his

AM BAHNHOF FRIEDRICHSTR.
AB 26. MAI TÄGL. 8³⁰ UHR
NUR KURZE ZEIT
GESAMTGASTSPIEL DER BERÜHMTEN

NEGER·PRODUCTION

CHOCOLATE KIDD
45 MITWIRKENDE
MIT
AMERIKAS
GRÖSSTEN FARBIGEN KÜNS
DIE LETZTE SENSATION A
ZUM ERSTEN MAL IN EUROPA
VORVERKAUF UNUNTERBROCHEN AN DER KASSE DES THEATER

Left: The Oranienplatz in 1926.
Above: Baselerstrasse at the corner of the Curtiusstrasse.
Lichterfelde West station is in the background.
Right: The Leipzigerstrasse in 1928.

Below left: The Alexanderplatz in 1925. It was named after
the Russian Tsar's visit in 1805. It was the point where
traffic coming from all directions met and was the most
hectic spot in Berlin.
Below: The Alexanderplatz railway station.

generation—violinists such as Fritz Kreisler (who was said to have been paid between 5000 and 8000 marks for one concert in contrast to Schnabel's 2500) and singers like Richard Tauber and Lotte Lehemann.

When Busoni died in 1924, the composer Arnold Schönberg took over his appointment and three years later Paul Hindemith was invited by Franz Schreker to take charge of a composition class at the Berlin Hochschule für Musik. One of his pupils, the Swiss harpsichordist Silvia Kind, left a sympathetic portrait of her master: 'Hindemith loved to organize hikes in the countryside with his class. Usually he would provide a huge joint for spit-roasting while we pupils had to bring the Stullen (large slices of bread and butter) as well as a round or canon composed by each of us for the sing-song. Hindemith was never annoyed by bad work, but he did not forgive me for a long time my failure to teach me a proper handstand or that his team lost a swimming race through me. . . . His great passion was the railway. He possessed about 900 yards of model railway track and the most sophisticated electric equipment with remote-control points and signals. . . . Frau Hindemith told us that Hindemith and his friends would often appear pale and exhausted at two or three in the morning and ask for schnaps, especially if Arthur (sic) Schnabel, another railway fanatic, was present.'

Schönberg, on the other hand, although having a passion for ping pong, to which a whole room was devoted in his flat on the Nürnberger Strasse, has been described as being in his fifty-first year a 'dour, irritable man . . . thin, bald-headed, asthmatic and embittered by years of hardship and opposition.' And certainly in his early years in Vienna he had found it difficult to find regular work, despite the interest shown in him by Richard Strauss, to whom he showed his monumental oratorio, the Gurrelieder, scored for five solo voices, four separate choruses and an orchestra of nearly 200 instruments, including a set of iron chains. In 1901 he accepted an offer from Ernst von Volzogen, who had developed a new type of cabaret chanson with his wife Laura, to be musical director and resident composer of their company, the Buntes Theater, which met in an art nouveau house. For them he set texts by Wedekind and Gustav Falke to music, but the collaboration did not last for more than three years and, disappointed, he returned to Vienna, where he taught harmony and counterpoint at a progressive grammar school.

Here in 1907–8 he composed his second string quartet, the last two movements of which included a part for soprano voice and a setting of some poems by Stefan George, in which, 'apart from final triadic cadences, tonality as such is rejected.' In his next work, Das Buch der Hangenden Garten, he broke away from tonality completely. 'Now,' wrote Schönberg, in a program note for the first per-

Left: Gustav Stresemann presents details of the Young Plan
to the Reichstag in 1929.
Above: Wilhelm Furtwängler became the conductor of the
Berlin Philharmonic on Kleiber's departure.
Right: Kurt Weill was also forced to emigrate to the United
States after 1933.

formance, 'I am aware of having broken through all the
barriers of a dated aesthetic ideal.'

Overflowing with ideas and creativity, Schönberg then
completed his controversial 500-page *Manual of Harmony*,
produced a number of oil paintings (much admired by
Wassily Kandinsky who arranged for them to be exhibited
at the Blaue Reiter), wrote his *Three Piano Pieces*, the *Five
Orchestral Pieces* and the strange, haunting *Erwartung*,
which consisted of three pieces for chamber orchestra and
six for the piano, each lasting for only a few moments.

Schönberg's arrival in Berlin caused something of a stir.
In 1923 he had gone even further in his experiments with
atonality with his twelve-tone or dodecaphonic technique,
in which the twelve notes of the chromatic scale were used
either as a melody or as harmony or counterpoint, and in
any order the composer chose. They could be turned inside
out, upside down or put back to front, as long as they con-
formed to the rule that no note was repeated unless it had
appeared in the original series.

Not everyone, however, was as excited by this new system
as Schönberg. Many felt it to be 'arid and cerebral' and
Thomas Mann thought it an invention of the Devil. (His
novel, *Dr Faustus*—by his own admission 'the intellectual
property of . . . Arnold Schönberg'—had as its central
character a composer who had invented a twelve-tone theory
and sold his soul to the Devil in order to ensure its success).
And when Schönberg's song cycle *Pierrot Lunaire* was

Above: The Red Front Fighters' League head office in 1930, when the Nazis and Communists were vying for control of Germany.
Below left: A leap for safety in front of the Zoo railway station in 1931.
Below far left: Advertisement for the Winter Garden Show in 1931.

performed in the Academy's auditorium on 5 January 1924 there was, according to one observer, 'a riot no less ferocious than the bedlam at the Paris premiere in 1913 of Igor Stravinsky's *Le Sacre du Printemps.* Some hotheads rose to condemn the "Jewish Bolshevism of Schönberg's caco-phonic garbage" and went on with tirades against the Weimar Republic, modern art, Schönberg, Jews, and music in general.'

Undeterred, Schönberg and his band of pupils who had accompanied him from Vienna continued to plumb the depths of musical experience in their efforts to find ever more satisfactory ways of expressing their ideas. Schön-berg's most famous pupil and his close friend, Alban Berg, stayed on in Vienna, pursuing his lonely and controversial path. He also had some trouble getting his work performed. In 1913 the second song of his *Altenberg Songs*—'Thunder-storm'—produced such an uproar the concert had to be abandoned, and at the subsequent court case a psychiatrist gave his opinion that 'music of this nature had a detrimental effect on the listener.'

Below: A sketch of Kurt Weill by Max Dungert in 1926.
Bottom: Gustav Stresemann is photographed.
Right: Sex or pornographic book shops were not unknown in Berlin before 1933.

All composers need sympathetic conductors. Berlin had attracted such giants as Wilhelm Furtwängler conducting the Berlin Philharmonic, Otto Klemperer, Leo Bloch, Georg Szell and Erich Kleiber sharing between them the two State Opera Houses and Bruno Walter directing the City Opera. Although basing their repertoire firmly on established favorites, all were active in promoting the work of their contemporaries. Furtwängler took an interest in Schönberg and persistently put his work before an uncomprehending but increasingly respectful public. Klem-

perer did Hindemith's *Cardillac* and Bruno Walter performed Leoš Janaček's *Katya Kabanova*, Bela Bartok's *Bluebeard's Castle* and introduced Dimitri Shostakovitch's *First Symphony* to Berlin.

But it was Erich Kleiber who caused the most sensational musical event of the mid-Twenties by subjecting Berlin audiences to the rigors of Alban Berg's opera, *Wozzeck*. By now, however, the concert-going public had a fair idea of what to expect. And, as one critic wrote hopefully '*Wozzeck* was suited to Berlin, in that it demanded of its audience a

constant alertness, an ability to "kiss the Joy as it flies," which few operas demand and few audiences possess.'

The libretto of *Wozzeck* was arranged by Berg himself from a play by Georg Büchner, the plot of which was highly melodramatic and redolent with heavy symbolism. It concerned the soldier Wozzeck, who, betrayed in love and taunted on all sides, murders his faithless mistress and commits suicide. Even Schönberg felt that the play was 'of such extraordinarily tragic power that it seemed forbidding to music' and advised his pupil to abandon the task of translating such scenes into musical terms. Berg, however, was adamant. The result was an extraordinary amalgam of oddly assorted technical devices. On the one hand he maintained a classical approach, using the suite, the rhapsody, the song, the march, the passacaglia and the rondo in the first act and a five-part symphony in the second. On the other hand he asked his soloists to intersperse their songs with ordinary speech and 'Sprechgesang' (half singing, half speaking) and he expected his chorus to snore. All this, however, in the opinion of one historian, combined with the gurgling of water, a tavern orchestra with an out-of-tune piano caricaturing a waltz motive from Strauss's *Rosenkavalier*, are skillfully employed for expressionistic purposes. The grim, ironical, symbolical action, the wealth of musical invention, the ever-varied ingenious and appropriate orchestration, the formal clarity and concentration, the pictorial quality and dramatic force of the music cumulate in an effect of unforgettable poignancy.'

It was originally thought that due to the exigencies of the score 137 'full' rehearsals would be required, and it was felt

that *Wozzeck* was beginning to occupy a disproportionate amount of the State Opera's time. In the end, however, only 34 rehearsals were needed for the piece, considered by Kleiber himself to be 'prodigiously difficult.' The news that the State Opera was producing a new work after so many years attracted a number of Berlin journalists who, as Kleiber's biographer recorded, 'clustered outside the darkened auditorium like buffaloes at a water hole. What could possibly be going on, they wondered?'

Berg came to Berlin to watch the rehearsals. He wrote copious letters to his wife in Vienna, telling her of the progress of his opera, alternating between extreme optimism and total despair. A week before the opening night he wrote, 'I am up sixteen to eighteen hours without a break. . . . How all of this—orchestra and stage—will be ready in eight days is beyond me, and I am comforted only by the conviction that Kleiber will not let anything unfinished out of his hands. He knows the success of the premiere depends on him. . . .'

In the event Berg need not have worried. The premiere

Right: Minister of the Interior, Carl Severing, leaves the polls in the 1932 presidential election.
Below: Nazis, Centrists, Social Democrats and Communists display their placards during 1932.

went off without a hitch. Kleiber, having heard that there was a possibility of organized opposition, and prepared for the worst, called his staff together beforehand and said, 'Well, if they make too much trouble we'll ring down the safety curtain and I'll do it just for you.' There was no need. The first-night audience, although divided in its reactions, was more or less in favor of the work. Hans Heinsheimer recorded that there were 'fist fights' and 'angry challenges' shouted across the orchestra seats, and from the boxes deriding boos, and hostile whistles that threatened for some time to overpower the small, but at last vigorous group of believers.' Surrounded by a combination of highly charged emotional excitement and hostility, both composer and conductor took their bows; 'we knew,' continued Heinsheimer, 'then and there, that we had been present at an historic event.'

As for the critics, they were surprisingly restrained. Apart from Paul Zschorlich of the *Deutsche Zeitung*, who felt he 'was not leaving a public place dedicated to the arts, but a public insane asylum,' all took the opera seriously and some allowed themselves a note of qualified approval. The Social-Democratic *Vorwärts* thought 'the hard logic of this drama was ennobled, humanized, psychologized through the spirit of music . . .' and even the conservative *Kreuz-Zeitung* wrote that in this opera Alban Berg had 'revealed himself as a progressive in the "moderate" sense of the word.'

For other composers, particularly those with affiliations to the *Novembergruppe*, opera was seen as a dying art form. Music, they felt, should express feeling without the handi-

Left: Nazi propaganda displayed during the Prussian state elections in 1932.
Below: Hindenburg and Hitler supporters in the first round of the presidential election in 1932.

cap of formal musical considerations. So when the jazz pianist 'Duke' Ellington appeared in Berlin in the summer of 1925 with his all-black revue, *Chocolate Kiddies*, it made a powerful impact on young Expressionist composers such as Ernst Krenek and Kurt Weill. Jazz, of course, was not new to Berlin—saxophones could be heard in nightclubs all over the city—but a full-length jazz show was something completely different.

Krenek, who had studied composition in Vienna under Frank Schreker, had followed his master to Berlin in 1920, where he joined his composition class at the Hochschule für Musik. In Berlin he came under the influence of Busoni, met and was befriended by the pianist Arthur Schnabel and married Gustav Mahler's daughter, Annie. He had written two operas, one of which, *Orpheus and Euridyce*, was a setting of an expressionistic libretto by the painter Oskar Kokoschka.

Chocolate Kiddies was, therefore, an intoxicating sight to the 25-year-old Krenek, not only because it liberated him from hitherto entrenched musical thought, but because it embodied the glittering, opportunist, materialistic world of America toward which inflation-ridden Germany cast her eyes so longingly. It inspired Krenek to embark on his jazz opera *Jonny Spielt Auf*, completed two years later and for which he wrote both the libretto and the music. The theme, which was 'jazz conquers all,' was interpreted through a series of catchy tunes and rhythms: the end result, an odd mixture of Puccini and Duke Ellington, had its premiere in Leipzig on 29 January 1927. It was first performed in Berlin on 21 November at the City Opera, where it caused great excitement.

Kurt Weill had also received a formal musical training, having been accepted as a member of Ferrucio Busoni's master class at the Berlin Academy in 1920. In 1924, however, he had written his *Concerto for Violin and Wind Band*, parts of which were heavily influenced by early jazz and the German dance music of the Twenties. One writer commented disapprovingly: 'Melodies and rhythms in a vulgar, popular idiom are consciously incorporated and a xylophone is given important solos.'

While on a visit to the Dresden Opera House in 1922 to hear Busoni's one-act opera, *Arlecchino*, Kurt Weill met the conductor, Fritz Busch, who later introduced him to the 'paramount dramatist of expressionism'—the violent and forthright playwright, poet and novelist, Georg Kaiser. Kaiser's most famous play was the horrifying and prophetic trilogy *Gas* (1920), which accurately forecast the use of the atom bomb—indeed most of his work was bound up with oppression and violence, either imposed or self-inflicted. He and Weill worked together on the one-act opera *The Protagonist*, a dark story set in the seventeenth century in which a brother murders his sister out of jealousy of her lover. While working on *The Protagonist* Weill lodged with the Kaiser family in their lakeside house at Grunheide outside Berlin. There he met the young Viennese dancer, Lotte Lenya. They fell in love and two years later they were married. Lotte Lenya recalled their first meeting: 'I took

Below: A Nazi trumpeter in 1932 Prussian elections.
Right: Communists demonstrate for their candidates in the Lustgarten. The Communist, Thälmann, ran a good third, but was imprisoned once Hitler came to power.

The square in front of the Potsdamer railway station in 1933,
the year Hitler took power.

the rowboat and went to the station and there was this funny-looking little man in great thick glasses and a little blue suit. "Would you mind entering the transportation?" I asked him. Our eyes met. We lived together for two years, and then I married Kurt Weill.'

Weill met the poet Bertolt Brecht in 1927 after he had found five of Brecht's *Mahagonny* poems; Brecht had written his own music for them, and Weill had elaborated on the original tunes. The resultant 'singspiel' was performed at the Festival of Chamber Music in Baden-Baden in June 1927. The staging was dramatic—against a stark black background workers paraded, carrying provocative socialist slogans. In the center of the stage was a boxing ring, in the middle of which stood Lotte Lenya singing her husband's music in her 'hoarse voice, with its lascivious inflections.' She herself remembered the occasion: 'I shall never forget the uproar which it caused. The audience rose to its feet and shouted approval, booed and whistled, simultaneously. Brecht had given us all little whistles and we simply whistled back at them.' It was Lotte Lenya's debut as a Brecht–Weill performer—one which she followed up a year later with her spectacular success as Pirate Jenny in *The Threepenny Opera*.

The uproar that accompanied the first performance of the 'singspiel' *Mahagonny* (known as *Das Kleine Mahagonny*) was nothing compared to that which followed the first night of the extended version—*The Rise and Fall of the City of Mahagonny*—which opened at the Leipzig Opera House on 9 March 1930. Loud jeering and cheering completely ruined the end of the performance, and the critic Alfred Polgar recorded that, 'Right next to me the following took place: The lady on my left was overcome by a heart-spasm and wanted to get out—and only the warning that this might prove a historic occasion kept her from leaving. The ancient Saxon on my right embraced his wife's knees and was overcome. A man behind me muttered to himself, "I'm only waiting for Brecht to turn up," and licked his chops.... Finally, *levée en masse* of the malcontents—but they in turn were discomfited by thunderous applause.... It was the first experiment of Brecht's epic theater, and the scandal which was unloosed already portended the approaching break up of the country.'

No wonder audiences were disturbed by *Mahagonny*. For it was, as Frederick Ewen aptly remarked, 'a provocation and was sensed as such by the bourgeois audience that responded articulately from its "bad conscience." They felt as if they were being attacked "by the united proletarians of all lands." The bourgeois heaven was being torn apart by sacrilegious hands, and its inner emptiness exposed. Gone was the feeling of good cheer that had greeted *The Threepenny Opera*, which could be taken as a jest. *Mahagonny* meant business.' For although supposedly set in America, the gold rush city of *Mahagonny*—turned during a typhoon into a nightmare of corruption, greed and lust, in which the ultimate crime was to be without money— was an all-too-recognizable portrait of Germany under the

Weimar Republic. The slogans carried by demonstrators in the final scene calling for 'the continuance of the age of gold.... For higher prices.... For chaos in our cities.... For the war of all against all,' were a searing and provocative indictment of the failure of the Weimar government to cure the running sores of inflation, unemployment and political instability.

Early in October 1929, three weeks before the Wall Street crash, Gustav Stresemann died, and Germany lost one of the few statesman with both the will and the intellect to combat the evils which beset her. As Foreign Minister Stresemann had negotiated the Dawes Plan in 1924 and the Young Plan, which reduced reparations to manageable proportions, had been largely responsible for the Treaty of Locarno, signed in 1925, which 'substituted for French military power a neutral zone in the Rhineland, guaranteed by Great Britain and Italy' and in 1926 piloted Germany into the League of Nations.

He left his country in the grip of mounting misery and unemployment and the Republic twitching in its own death throes. After the collapse of the coalition government of Hermann Müller on 27 March 1930, President Hindenburg asked Heinrich Brüning, formerly chairman of the Center delegation to the Reichstag, to form an administration. He embarked on a series of stringent anti-inflationary policies, designed to boost conservative morale but devastating for the workers. Despite these conciliatory right-wing gestures, he failed to win the support of the Nazi Party, who took to the streets 'in defiance of police orders,' where they came into open conflict with Communists. Berlin was once more

Left: A working class alley seems divided in its support of Nazis and Communists in 1932.
Right: Dr Josef Goebbels, master propagandist of the Nazi Party and architect of its success.

Previous page: Strikers erect barricades in 1932.
Above: Naval troops help police suppress rioting near the
Brandenburg Gate in 1932.
Below: Hitler's Shadow Cabinet in 1932. From left to right:
Dr Dietrich, Putzi Hanfstängl, Hermann Göring, Adolf Hitler,
Ernst Röhm and Dr Frick.
Right: Chancellor Hitler and Vice-Chancellor von Papen in
Potsdam during January 1933.

a city of insurrection—barricades were once more across the streets and armed snipers faced each other from both sides. And Joseph Goebbels, appointed by Hitler Gauleiter of Berlin in 1926, rallied his increasing number of supporters at mass rallies. 'There was a rally in Friedrichshain,' wrote one Nazi, 'The speaker was Dr Goebbels. There were 5000 people inside the park, another 3000 outside. And everything was nice and peaceful, only a few small disturbances every so often out on the street.' Unwisely, however, the police keeping an eye on the rally issued orders through a loud hailer that no shouts of 'Heil' would be allowed, and, when the inevitable happened, 'immediately lost their nerve and attacked the crowd with truncheons. . . . There was shouting and screaming and confusion and pushing. . . .'

Brüning, in the face of persistent opposition, was unable to persuade the Reichstag to approve his financial measures. In July 1930 he dissolved the Reichstag and called for national elections. Re-elected by a narrow majority Brüning returned to head the government, but Nazi gains had been immense—they had increased their number of Reichstag seats from twelve to 107. The elections, however, did nothing to change the plight of the people. Hindenburg 'signed one emergency decree after another, controlling the price of food, regulating bank payments, reducing unem-

ployment compensations,' but to no avail. Germany needed a savior—and unfortunately Adolf Hitler, with his extraordinary powers of oratory and capacity to generate physical excitement, had persuaded a large section of the country during his election campaign in 1930 that he was just such a deliverer.

Emboldened by their successes at the polls, the Nazis became increasingly vociferous and militant. Fanned by propaganda from the Nazi press, skillfully manipulated by Joseph Goebbels, party fanatics began to militate actively against Communists and Jews. 'The Jew,' shouted Goebbels to ever-larger rallies, 'is the real demon of destruction. . . . We are the enemies of Jews because we identify ourselves as Germans. The Jew is our greatest curse. But this will change, as surely as we are Germans.'

Nazis were even found to have infiltrated the Reichswehr—expressly forbidden by the Army since 1927—and in September 1930 three young lieutenants were put on trial for treason, accused of 'enlisting fellow officers to the Nazi cause.' Hitler spoke in their defense, using the witness box as a convenient forum to reassure the Army that his Stormtroopers had no designs on them: 'None of us have any interest in replacing the Army. . . . We will see to it when we come to power, that out of the present Reichswehr a great Army of the German people shall arise.' He also told the court that the Nazi Party had no desire to seize power by unconstitutional means. Hitler was, however, addressing the army, whose support was crucial to the fulfillment of his all-consuming lust for power, and he avoided mentioning that constitutions could be manipulated or altered by their guardians.

So convincing was he that many army officers began to feel that perhaps National Socialism was, after all, just what the country needed. The translation of mood into substance was, however, a different matter. The unwitting midwife of the Third Reich was the slippery Major General Kurt von Schleicher, a General Staff Officer of more than usually calculating temperament. He set himself the task of reconciling the Nazi Party to the existing regime—persuading President Hindenburg, whose son, Oskar, was a friend of his, that it was in the country's interests as Alan Bullock put it, to convert 'the Nazi movement with its mass following into a prop of the existing government, instead of a battering ram directed against it.'

Hitler, in his turn, was prepared to use his mass support as the trump card in his bid to secure power and recognition within the Reichstag. Early in the autumn of 1931 General von Schleicher had a meeting with Hitler, and subsequently persuaded Hindenburg and Brüning to see him. The interview with Hindenburg was not a success. 'He was,' the President considered, 'a queer fellow, who would never make a Chancellor, but, at most, a Minister of Posts.'

Nevertheless, despite the President's reservations, membership of the Nazi party showed no sign of slackening—between January and December 1931 it increased from 389,000 to 800,000. General von Schleicher was more convinced than ever that the Nazis should be 'made use of' and even managed to win over the stubbornly anti-Nazi Minister of Defense, General Gröner, putting it to him that if this was not wholly desirable, it was probably inevitable.

The Hardenbergstrasse in the winter of 1932–33 when
Hitler took power.

Left: The Alexanderplatz and Wertheim's department store in 1931. Wertheim's was seized in 1933 because of its Jewish ownership.
Bottom left: The Alexanderplatz in 1933 just after the Nazi take over.
Above: The Friedrichstrasse in 1932.
Below: The Alexanderplatz from the Neuen Königstrasse in 1932.

Hitler's response to these overtures was tempered by an outspoken desire to get rid of Chancellor Brüning—whom he blamed unequivocally for the ills of the republic. Early in 1932 the question of extending President Hindenburg's term of office cropped up. After consultations with the Nazis—whose headquarters had become the Kaiserhof Hotel—Hindenburg agreed to stand for re-election, and Hitler, after some initial hesitation, allowed himself to be persuaded to stand against him. The first ballot failed to give Hindenburg an absolute majority and a run-off was necessary. On 10 April 1932 Hindenburg achieved an absolute majority with nineteen million votes, Hitler coming a close second with thirteen and a half million. A month later, on the advice of General von Schleicher, the President dismissed the Brüning Cabinet. The new Chancellor was the 'smooth, gaunt, manipulative, reactionary Centrist, Franz von Papen' and the new Minister of Defense Kurt von Schleicher. The road to barbarism had begun.

The events of the following year followed one upon another with dispiriting inevitability. The July elections brought the Nazis overwhelming gains. Von Papen offered Hitler Nazi positions in the government, but Hitler wanted the Chancellorship or nothing. Hamstrung, von Papen dissolved the Reichstag and once more the long-suffering German public was obliged to go to the polls. This time the Nazis did less well—the more overt manfestations of Nazi policy had not been lost on the public, who were beginning to suspect that the open brutality of Nazi speech and action might be too high a price to pay for economic stability. It was a low moment for the Nazi Party. Financial backing was fitful, Goebbels 'feared for the future' and Hitler 'darkly hinted at suicide.' At this point Kurt von Schleicher played conveniently into their hands.

After the elections of November 1932, von Papen once more offered to negotiate with Hitler. Hitler, however, flatly refused to deal with him at all—Papen, he declared, 'was driving the masses to Bolshevism' and there could be no compromise with him. Infuriated, von Papen was prepared to go once again to the polls, to 'force the Nazis to their knees'; but he was opposed by Schleicher, who, irritated by the close relationship that existed between von Papen and President Hindenburg, and seeing his plan to accommodate the Nazis peaceably within the existing framework slipping from his grasp, appealed to the Cabinet for support. It was agreed that von Papen should be suspended in order to allow the President to 'consult the Party leaders and try and find a way out of the deadlock.' None, however, was found and most reluctantly President Hindenburg was forced to accept his favorite's resignation. In his place the scheming General von Schleicher had the doubtful distinction of becoming the last Chancellor of pre-Hitler Germany.

He had, however, underestimated both the depth of von Papen's dislike for himself and the extent of his desire to return to power. Suddenly Schleicher, the arch-intriguer, found himself at the center of a network of plots and counter-plots. Hitler allied himself with the ousted von Papen instead of with his own administration, for von Papen had managed to persuade Hindenburg that should Hitler become Chancellor he could be kept in check by himself

as Vice-Chancellor and 'other reliable conservatives in the Cabinet.'

Outwitted, Schleicher resigned, and in a blissful state of senile trust in his protegé, the old President agreed to offer the Chancellorship to Hitler. On 30 January 1933 'after a sleepless night during which he sat up with Göring and Goebbels to be ready for any eventuality,' Hitler was summoned to see the President. 'During the morning,' wrote Alan Bullock, 'a silent crowd filled the street between the Kaiserhof and the Chancellery. . . . Shortly after noon a roar went up from the crowd: . . . the improbable had happened: Adolf Hitler, the petty official's son from Austria, the down-and-out of the Home for Men, the Meldegänger of the List Regiment, had become Chancellor of the Third Reich.' Darkness had come to the City of Mahagonny.

The night Hitler took power, 30 January 1933.
Above: Cheering crowds hail the new Führer.
Right: The torchlight parade through the Brandenburg Gate.
Below: Hitler at the window of the Reichschancellery.

The burning of the books. Nazi supporters destroy
'un-German' literature at the Opernplatz in 1933. This
included the work of Communists, many socialists and Jews.

STADT MAHAGONNY

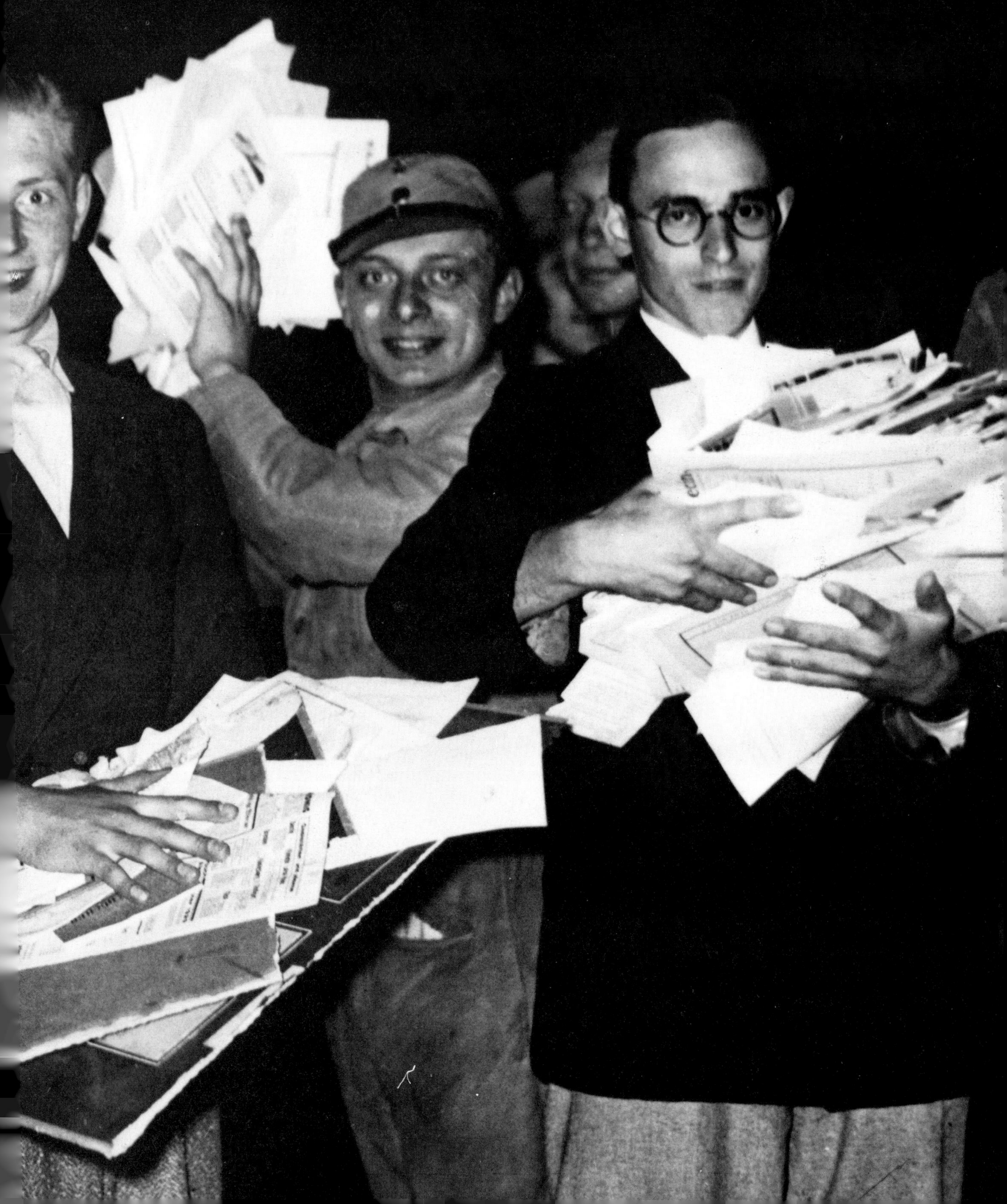

'I miss the old Berlin of the Republic,' wrote William Shirer in his diary on 2 September 1934, 'the carefree, emancipated, civilized air, the snub-nosed young women with short bobbed hair and the young men with either cropped or long hair—it made no difference—who sat up all night with you and discussed anything with intelligence and passion.' The carefree days had indeed gone. The climate was still the best in the world, the air was as clear as ever, but the atmosphere of intellectual and sexual freedom that had brought W H Auden, Stephen Spender and Christopher Isherwood to Berlin in the late Twenties, had been swept away in a welter of Heil Hitlers, clicking of heels and brown-shirted stormtroopers or black-coated SS Guards marching up and down the streets.'

Christopher Isherwood, whose collection of autobiographical sketches *Mr Norris Changes Trains* and *Goodbye to Berlin* drew an unforgettable portrait of the city and its inhabitants, was lured there in the first place by his friend, Auden—and, as Otto Friedrich pointed out, 'not just for the climate.' He wanted to find out if a relative of his, a Hamburg shipping merchant, was right when he denounced Berlin as being full of 'shameless rituals of the Tantras' and perversions worse than anything the 'oriental' mind could conceive, and whether, in fact the city was 'doomed, more surely than Sodom ever was.'

He found a series of contradictions—a city with 'two centers—the cluster of expensive hotels, bars, cinemas, shops round the Memorial Church ... and the self-conscious civic center of building round the Unter den Linden, carefully arranged' but 'the real heart of Berlin was in a small damp wood—the Tiergarten.' He found glitter and decay, riches and poverty, extremes of heat and extremes of cold. 'Berlin is a skeleton,' he wrote in *A Berlin Diary*, written in the winter of 1932–33, 'which aches in the cold. It is my own skeleton aching. I feel in my bones the sharp ache of the frost in the girders of the overhead railway, in the ironwork of balconies, in bridges, tramlines, lamp-standards, latrines. The iron throbs and shrinks, the stone and the bricks ache dully, the plaster is numb.'

Isherwood lodged in a tenement block in a working-class area, living off 'the food of the poor, horse meat and lung soup.' The first meal that his landlady in the Wassertorstrasse, the immortal Frau Nowak, cooked him was lung hash—which, her son, Otto, told him was a particular treat. He was visited by Stephen Spender, who was not as well-disposed toward the place as his friend: '. . . the gray houses whose façades seemed out of molds made for the pressing of enormous concrete biscuits. . . . A peculiar and all-pervading smell of hopeless decay . . . came out of the interiors of these grandiose houses now converted into pretentious slums.' One of Isherwood's most endearing qualities was his capacity for affection—his portraits of landladies, girls, and young men, whether rich or poor, Jew or Communist, were never less than sympathetic. He made a uniquely English contribution to the galaxy of recollections of Berlin in the Twenties—understated, delicately restrained and with a keen eye for the ridiculous. In *A Berlin Diary* he described a confrontation between a Communist and some Stormtroopers:

'A young Communist I know was arrested by the SA men, taken to a Nazi barracks, and badly knocked about. After

Above: The first official document signed by Hitler creating his new government.

three or four days, he was released and went home. Next morning there was a knock at the door. The Communist hobbled over to open it, his arm in a sling—and there stood a Nazi with a collecting-box. At the sight of him the Communist completely lost his temper. "Isn't it enough," he yelled, "that you beat me up? And you dare to come and ask me for money?" But the Nazi only grinned. "Now, now, comrade! No political squabbling! Remember, we're living in the Third Reich! We're all brothers! You must try and drive that silly political hatred from your heart!"' It was a far cry from the desperate involvement of Bertolt Brecht or the tortured introspection of George Grosz.

Another, but more emotional, expatriate living in Berlin at that time was the writer Vladimir Nabokov, who spent a total of fourteen years in the city. His father, a former member of the Russian parliament, had come to Germany after the revolution, as had many other right-wing Russian emigres. 'The Russian colony in Berlin in the Twenties was quite large,' said one commentator, 'perhaps fifty thousand, perhaps more. . . . And it was not just intellectuals. It was a world in itself. There were doctors, lawyers, businessmen. There were several very good tennis players . . . we had two Russian soccer teams in Berlin. . . .' With them they

Top right: Hitler's Cabinet in a weekly magazine.
Bottom right: The new cabinet. Seated, Göring, Hitler and von Papen. Standing, Schwerin-Krosigk, Frick, von Blomberg and Hügenberg.

GEDENKAUSGABE DER WOCHE

Das Kabinett der nationalen Erneuerung

Links: Adolf Hitler
seit dem 30. Januar 1933
deutscher Reichskanzler
und Führer des Kabinetts
der nationalen Erneue-
rung, das bei der Reichs-
tagswahl am 5. März durch
eine überwältigende Mehr-
heit die Zustimmung des
Volkes erhielt

Rechts:
Vizekanzler
Franz v. Papen

Dr. Alfred Hugenberg
Reichsminister für Wirtschaft und Ernährung

Franz Seldte
Reichsarbeitsminister

Konstantin Freiherr v. Neurath
Reichsminister des Auswärtigen

Dr. Joseph Goebbels
Reichsminister für Volksaufklärung

Lutz Graf Schwerin v. Krosigk
Reichsminister der Finanzen

Paul Freiherr v. Eltz-Rübenach
Reichsminister für Post und Verkehr

Dr. Franz Gürtner
Reichsminister der Justiz

Hermann Göring
Reichsminister für Luftverkehr

Werner Freiherr v. Blomberg
Reichswehrminister

Dr. Wilhelm Frick
Reichsminister des Innern

Nazis march in front of Communist headquarters, Karl Liebknecht House, in January 1933. It was closed soon after Hitler's takeover. The poster reads: In Your Spirit, Forward in the Struggle against the Danger of War, Fascism, Hunger and Frost, for Work, Bread and Freedom. The pictures on the right are of Lenin, Liebknecht and Luxemburg.

brought borscht, caviar, blinis and shashlik and in the restaurants and cabarets (the Coq d'Or, the Blue Bird, the Bear, the Allaverdi) the sound of the balalaika filled the air. Congregating within these monuments to their homeland were talented Russians like the cellist Gregor Piatigorsky, the singer Boris Chaliapin, the painter Wassily Kandinsky and the poet Mayakovsky. Maxim Gorki and Ilya Ehrenburg were also in Berlin, as was Vladimir Horowitz, who gave a concert in 1925, and the dancer Isadora Duncan, who brought her young husband, the 'brilliant but half-demented' poet, Sergei Essenin.

Nabokov lived entirely among this Russian community. By his own admission he spoke no German, had no German friends and had 'not read a single German novel either in the original or in translation.' He made his living by giving tennis and English lessons—he also translated *Alice in Wonderland* into Russian and devised, for his father's newspaper, the first Russian crossword puzzle. His early novels were a direct reflection of this isolation from his new surroundings and drew a vivid picture of the enclosed, expatriate, Russian world—that strange mixture of 'tea, intrigue and . . . interminable poetry readings'—in which he lived.

The existence in Berlin during the Twenties of so many oddly assorted elements—White Russians, Red Russians, German Communists, German Nationalists, and German Jews mixed up with a smattering of English or Americans

Left: President von Hindenburg leaves the polling station on the day of the Reichstag election of March 1933.
Below left: Communists are rounded up by the SA in Berlin the day after the Reichstag election.
Below: Hindenburg and Hitler ride to the Lustgarten to celebrate the Day of National Work, 1 May 1933.

was one of the city's greatest charms and contributed directly to its extraordinary cultural diversity. Its attractions for talents as varied as the scientist Albert Einstein, whose theory of relativity, according to one historian, 'changed the world even more profoundly than two world wars,' the Communist theoretician Rosa Luxemburg, the architect Walter Gropius and the controversial composer Arnold Schönberg, were manifold: only in Berlin was there so much hunger for the new, so fierce a rejection of the old, and so much intellectual and artistic freedom to translate these new ideas into reality.

It was one of the Third Reich's many crimes that it committed not only physical but artistic murder. The cultural world of Weimar died with the proclamation of Adolf Hitler as Chancellor and with it died the hope and the freedom of Germany. Propaganda took the place of experimentation, bigotry replaced freedom of expression and sentimentality triumphed over satire. No wonder William Shirer was depressed.

For a time many people refused to acknowledge that their new leader was as bad as he seemed. True, he fulminated against the Jews, but once he had time to think things over he would realize that the Jews were the backbone of the country. They could not believe, like Bernard Landauer, in Christopher Isherwood's story, *The Landauers*, that the threats were real. When Bernard received an anonymous letter, saying 'Bernard Landauer, beware. We are going to settle the score with you and your uncle and all other filthy Jews. We give you 24 hours to leave Germany. If not, you are dead men,' he laughed it off as the work of a practical joker or a madman. Later he died mysteriously of 'heart failure.'

And when Hitler railed against the Communists, many

Berlin police parade the swastika flag in 1933. By this time the Nazi takeover was virtually complete.

remembered that there had nearly been a 'Bolshevik' revolution in 1919 and reminded themselves that they could not be too careful. After all Germany was badly in need of a strong hand to guide her through those difficult days when jobs were scarce and money was tight. Joseph Goebbels voiced the unconscious wishes of many when he wrote in his diary on 31 January 1933: 'In a conference with the Führer we lay down the line for the fight against the Red terror. For the moment we shall abstain from direct countermeasures. The Bolshevik attempt at revolution must first burst into flame. At the proper moment we shall strike.'

Below: Nazis file past the Reichstag in a funeral service for those who died fighting Communists in the streets, during the most violent clashes in 1933.

The revolution, however, showed no signs of coming. But at about 9.10 pm on the night of 27 February 1933 a 21-year-old typesetter called Werner Thaler was passing the Reichstag building when he heard the sound of breaking glass. He ran back to find a policeman, shouting: 'Quick. Someone's trying to break into the Reichstag.'

'For a moment,' wrote Fritz Tobias, historian of the Fire, 'all three of them looked on in paralyzed astonishment. Then, as the man could be seen rushing from window to window waving a flaming torch, the three men started after him.' There followed a desperate attempt to shoot him, but after firing a few abortive shots into the building, the policeman asked a second bystander to alert the Brandenburg Gate police guardroom and get them to rouse the fire brigade. It was, however, too late to save the building. Vice-Chancellor von Papen was having dinner with

President Hindenburg at the Herrenklub, just around the corner from the Reichstag. 'Suddenly,' he later recorded, 'we noticed a red glow through the windows and heard sounds of shouting in the street. One of the servants came hurrying up to me and whispered: "The Reichstag is on fire!" which I repeated to the President. He got up and from the window we could see the dome of the Reichstag looking as though it were illuminated by searchlights. Every now and again a burst of flame and a swirl of smoke blurred the outline.'

By 11.00 pm the fire was under control, but the building was a blackened, gutted wreck. Earlier in the evening, however, the pyromaniac had been arrested, caught running from the flaming Session Chamber into the corridor beyond and had been taken away to the Brandenburg Gate Police headquarters. His name was Marinus van der Lubbe and he came from Leyden in Holland.

Whether the Reichstag fire was the work of van der Lubbe on his own, whether he was the dupe of the Nazis, a Communist, a homosexual, a congenital idiot or a pathological liar, has been the subject of considerable debate. Whatever the exact truth, the Nazis used the event as a pretext in their move toward large-scale political repression. The day after the fire, as William Shirer said, the govern-

Left: After the Reichstag Fire this paper asked: It is burning; who will put it out?
Below: The line of march for the 1 May parade in 1933. Note the change of street names, eg Horst Wessel-Platz.

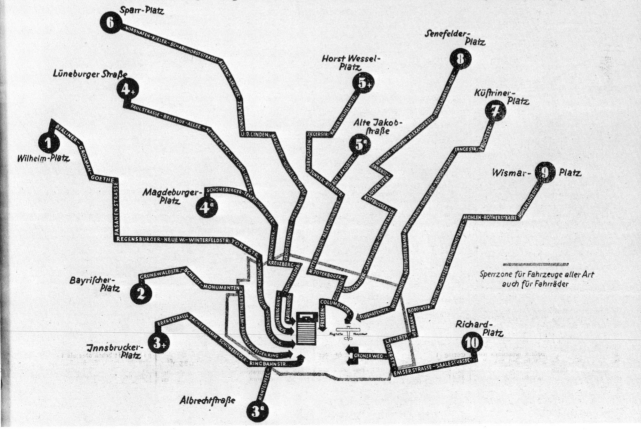

Aufmarschplan zum 1. Mai.

So marschieren die Kolonnen am „Feiertag der nationalen Arbeit" aus allen Stadtteilen zum Tempelhofer Feld.

Above: The Reichstag aflame.
Inset right: Marinus van de Lubbe, who was accused of setting the building on fire. Historians now agree that van der Lubbe was the arsonist, but the Nazis made political capital from the incident.

Above: Berlin weekly shows the Army parade down the Unter den Linden on Memorial Day in 1933.
Above right: The opening of the Reichstag.

ment issued a statement, declaring that it had found Communist 'documents' proving that 'Government buildings, museums, mansions and essential plants were to be burned down. . . . Women and children were to be sent in front of terrorist groups. . . . The burning of the Reichstag was to be the signal for a bloody insurrection and civil war. . . .' Small wonder that in the ensuing general elections, the last during Hitler's lifetime, the Communists dropped a million votes. The new Reichstag, in which the government had a small majority of sixteen seats, was opened on 21 March 1933 in the Garrison Church at Potsdam. Two days later the Reichstag convened in the Kroll Opera House, Berlin, where the delegates were asked to approve the 'so-called Enabling Act—the "Law for Removing the Distress of People and Reich,"' which in effect transferred control of the budget, approval of treaties with foreign states and the initiation of constitutional amendments away from Parliament and placed them under the control of the Reich cabinet. To their credit the Social Democrats stood resolutely against such draconian measures and voted unanimously against the bill. Support from the center party, however, turned the scales in the Nazis' favor and the bill was approved by 441 to 84. 'Thus,' wrote William Shirer, 'was parliamentary democracy finally interred in Germany.'

After that it became apparent even to the most optimistic that Germany was no place for any but the compliant. It was certainly no place for political or racial deviants. The day after the Reichstag fire Bertolt Brecht escaped from

Berlin to Prague. From there he wandered around the world 'in an eternal search for another Berlin, which he found again in 1949.' In Copenhagen he wrote a poem, the last lines of which were:

'Lucretius went into exile
So did Heine, and so
Under the straw roofs of Denmark fled Brecht.'

Kurt Weill and Lotte Lenya made for Paris, as did Wassily Kandinsky. Kurt Tucholsky went to Sweden, where later he committed suicide. Käthe Kollwitz, although expelled from the Royal Academy, stayed on—in the following years she made eight large lithographs which she called 'Death.'

Albert Einstein was no stranger to anti-Semitism. An ardent Zionist, he had encountered nationalist prejudice in the mid-Twenties. 'Some of these Nationalists,' wrote Otto Friedrich, 'took to waiting for Einstein outside his apartment on the Haberlandstrasse, or his office in the Prussian Academy of Science, and shouting denunciations of "Jewish science" as soon as the familiar figure appeared. Others filled his mailbox with obscene and threatening letters. On one occasion, a gang of right-wing students disrupted Einstein's lecture at the Berlin University, and one of them shouted, "I'm going to cut the throat of that dirty Jew." . . .' Germany's loss was California's gain. He went there to teach at the California Institute of Technology in 1930 and although he returned spasmodically to Berlin, he left for good two years later.

As for George Grosz, the very nature of whose art was particularly offensive to National Socialist sensibilities, he endured persistent persecution from the Brownshirts between 1930 and 1933. In 1932 he accepted an invitation

Nummer 13. 31. März 1932.   Berliner   41. Jahrgang. Preis 20 Pfennig

Illustrirte Zeitung

Verlag Ullstein Berlin SW 68

Eine Film-Sensation: Greta Garbo und Marlene Dietrich als siamesische Zwillinge
in dem neuen Film „Tragödie einer Liebe".

Die beiden Künstlerinnen sind den größten Film-Ruhm der Welt gelangt durch ihre
gemeinsame Gestaltung als siamese Doppel-Künstlerische Darstellung

---

Sonnabend, den 14. Jan., 23¹⁄₂ Uhr

Wohltätigkeits - Vorstellung des Schutzverbandes
Deutscher Schriftsteller in der

SCALA

Nacht-Parade

Felix Bressart
Hilde Hildebrand
Edith Lorand und ihr Orchester
Rudolf Nelson
Asta Nielsen
Max Pallenberg
Willi Schaeffers und
das gesamte Scala - Programm

Es konferieren:

Wolfgang Goetz	Anton Kuh
Fritz Grünbaum	Heinrich Mann
Walter Hasenclever	Walter von Molo
Walter von Hollander	Roda Roda
Alfred Kerr	Carl Zuckmayer

Leitung: **Peter Sachse**

Eintrittskarten zum Preise von 80 Pf. bis RM 4,— in
der Scala u. allen bekannten Billetverkaufsstellen

Left: Weekly magazine shows Garbo and Dietrich as Siamese twins in a film *Tragedy of Love*.

to teach at the Art Students' League in New York, but returning to Berlin in October of that year he received 'frequent anonymous telephone calls from the SA.' Beth Lewis gave an account of one such call:

'"Listen, you Jewish swine, tomorrow night we are coming and slaughtering you and all your brood."

"Just come" shouted Grosz into the telephone, "I have two pistols, my wife also has two, and my friend Uli has a Basque walking stick with a bayonet! We'll show you what's what!"'

Grosz remained defiant, but a realization of what the future might hold for him and his wife made him emigrate to America on 12 January 1933. On 27 February, the day of the Reichstag fire, Grosz's empty Berlin apartment was searched. 'He was certain,' wrote Mrs Lewis, 'that if he had been there, he would not have come out alive.' In the event, in his absence, on 8 March 1933 he was officially deprived of his German citizenship. Later he was accused by the Nazi regime of being 'one of the most evil representatives of degenerate art who worked in a manner which was hostile to Germany.'

Arnold Schönberg also became 'undesirable,' both as a Jew and as an exponent of 'degenerate' music. While working on his opera *Moses and Aron* in Paris in 1933, he received a message from Berlin announcing that his life appointment at the Prussian Academy of Arts had been terminated, without any legal justification. After a short stay in Paris Schönberg accepted an appointment to the Malkin Conservatory in New York and Boston, but like many others left all his worldly goods in Germany—'life,' as one historian said 'was a hard struggle for the sixty-year-old composer. The state of his health was unpredictable, but his sense of purpose was undiminished.' But in 1947, awarded the one thousand dollar prize of the American Academy of Arts, Schönberg actually paid tribute to his oppressors—saying that he had 'felt what it was like to fall into an ocean of boiling water.' His virtue 'had been that he had not given up, but had struggled on. His opponents deserved to be thanked, because in fact they had helped him.' Other musicians suffered a similar fate.

In the summer of 1933 Fritz Busch left Germany 'after a series of indignities at Dresden,' Otto Klemperer had his Berlin contract cancelled 'at a moment's notice,' and Bruno Walter had left the country in protest at the prevailing climate of repression. Erich Kleiber stayed on until 1935 battling against jibes, on the one hand that he was a Jew, and on the other that he was an anti-Semite. His rivals swore he stayed to make a bargain with the Nazis; his friends saw him as a champion of the Jewish cause. His loyalty to Alban Berg remained unswerving. He tried to get Berg's opera *Lulu*, completed in 1934, performed at the Berlin State Opera but without success. Berg himself was fully aware

Left: Advertisement for the Scala in 1933. Soon afterward many of the writers and artists had emigrated.
Right: Cartoon hailing the Day of National Labor, 1 May 1933. May Day, with its Socialist overtones was abolished and replaced by a Nazi festival.

of the difficulties. He wrote to Kleiber saying that as a compromise he 'was going to devise an orchestral suite of about 25 minutes' duration out of *Lulu*. . . . Would you, could you, and are you brave enough to, give the first of all these performances? From what Furtwängler says I think that we could risk doing it even in Germany.'

In May 1934 Mrs Kleiber (whose husband was then in Brussels) had an interview with Hermann Göring 'to discuss the matter of *Lulu*.' She was kept waiting for three-quarters of an hour. When she finally came into his presence 'he sat silently . . . tapping his desk with a pencil eighteen inches long. "You've come about Berg," he said at last. "Berg. A Jew, isn't he?" "No," said Mrs Kleiber, "He's not a Jew." "Well, what about him anyway? Why does your husband want to do his music? I hear it's no good." Mrs Kleiber, hypnotized by the Minister's painted finger nails and rouged face managed to rally her wits. "It's a matter of life and death to my husband that this music should be performed. He doesn't ask you to approve it. He just asks for protection during the performance—so that it shouldn't be interrupted. That's all." ' Göring, possibly remembering the one and only time Kleiber had given the Nazi salute (at a performance of *Siegfried*, when he did it for a bet) was surprisingly agreeable. The performance took place on 30 November 1934—it was, as John Russell remarked, 'in the nature of a last salute to the independent, free-tongued, inquisitive Berlin of the 1920s.'

Left: Wertheim's sale in 1933. The largest department store in Berlin was taken over by the Nazis.
Below: A selection of 1933 bathing suits.

During the evening a demonstrator sprang to his feet, shouting, 'Heil Mozart!' Kleiber replied: 'You are mistaken, the piece was by Alban Berg.' Four days later he resigned his post. 'It was impossible,' he said, 'to carry on in a country where music was not, like air and sunlight, free to all.' Göring tried to persuade him to change his mind —offering him any salary he liked 'payable in Swiss francs to an account anywhere in the world.' Kleiber answered that he would come back on condition he could give a Mendelssohn program for his first concert. Needless to say, he heard nothing more. He did not return to Berlin until 1951, when he conducted *Der Rosenkavalier* in the Admiralspalast.

The first year of Hitler's reign as Chancellor was a honeymoon of extraordinary harmony and peace. In it he had, as William Shirer neatly put it, 'overthrown the Weimar Republic, substituted his personal dictatorship for its democracy, destroyed all the political parties but his own, smashed the state governments and their parliaments, . . . wiped out the labor unions, stamped out democratic associations of any kind, driven the Jews out of public and professional life, abolished freedom of speech and of the press, stifled the independence of the courts and "co-ordinated" under Nazi rule the political, economic, cultural and social life of an ancient and cultivated people.' There remained, however, one problem—that of the Stormtroopers.

By the end of 1933 the SA under their Chief of Staff, Ernst Röhm, had swollen to more than two million men, and their existence posed a positive threat to the Reichswehr. The ambitious Röhm, his force now twenty times

Zweiteiliger Schwimm- und Strandanzug mit modischen Rippen. Das weitgeschnittene Höschen wird über dem Badeanzug mit einem Gummigürtel befestigt und zum Baden ausgezogen.

Neue Form des Badeanzuges mit breitem Gürtel, der es ermöglicht, den Rückenausschnitt beliebig zu verändern. Der gute Sitz wird durch die wie ein Büstenhalter gearbeitete Schnittlinie erreicht.

Hitler, Hindenburg and Göring at the Tannenberg Memorial
on 27 August 1933.

Above: Reichstag election poster in November 1933 urges voters to support the Marshal and the Corporal.

Above: Hitler returns to a cheering throng at the Reichschancellery after a meeting with Hindenburg.

larger than the regular army, felt that the SA should be recognized as the 'revolutionary army' of the new Germany. Hitler, however, was for a number of reasons unwilling to renege on his promises made to the Reichswehr in 1930— one being that only the generals of the old guard had the technical skills needed to plan and implement German rearmament. Therefore, in order to appease his power-hungry colleague, he took Röhm into the Cabinet and, to placate the Army, he offered to reduce the Stormtroopers' numbers.

Röhm, however, had enemies other than the Reichswehr generals. Heinrich Himmler, commander of the elite SS, and Hermann Göring, recently made a general, who had the Berlin police under his command (a 'special section' of which he kept at the Lichterfelde Cadet School) were both deeply suspicious of the SA in general and Röhm in particular. Between them they managed to convince Hitler that Röhm and the SA were involved in a plot against him. It was apparently Himmler who finally forced Hitler to acknowledge that there was some truth in the rumor that

his old comrade wanted to stage a *Putsch*. But the army too became caught up in the tangled web of plot and counter-plot that surrounded Berlin and decided that Röhm must go—but, as one historian pointed out, although 'pressing for a purge . . . it did not want to soil its own hands. That must be done by Hitler, Göring and Himmler, with their black-coated SS and Göring's special police.'

Although Hitler said later that all he wanted was to 'deprive the chief of staff of his office . . . and arrest a number of SA leaders whose crimes were unquestioned . . .' the end result was very different. Not only was it a purge of supposed malcontents within the SA but it was a blood-thirsty reckoning of old scores that had little or nothing to do with the suspected *Putsch*.

On the morning of 30 June 1934 Ernst Röhm and the leader of the Munich SA, Lieutenant Edmund Heines, were asleep in their rooms at the Hanselbauer Hotel at

Right: Professor Adolf Ziegler after his appointment as president of the Reichs Chamber for Graphic Art.

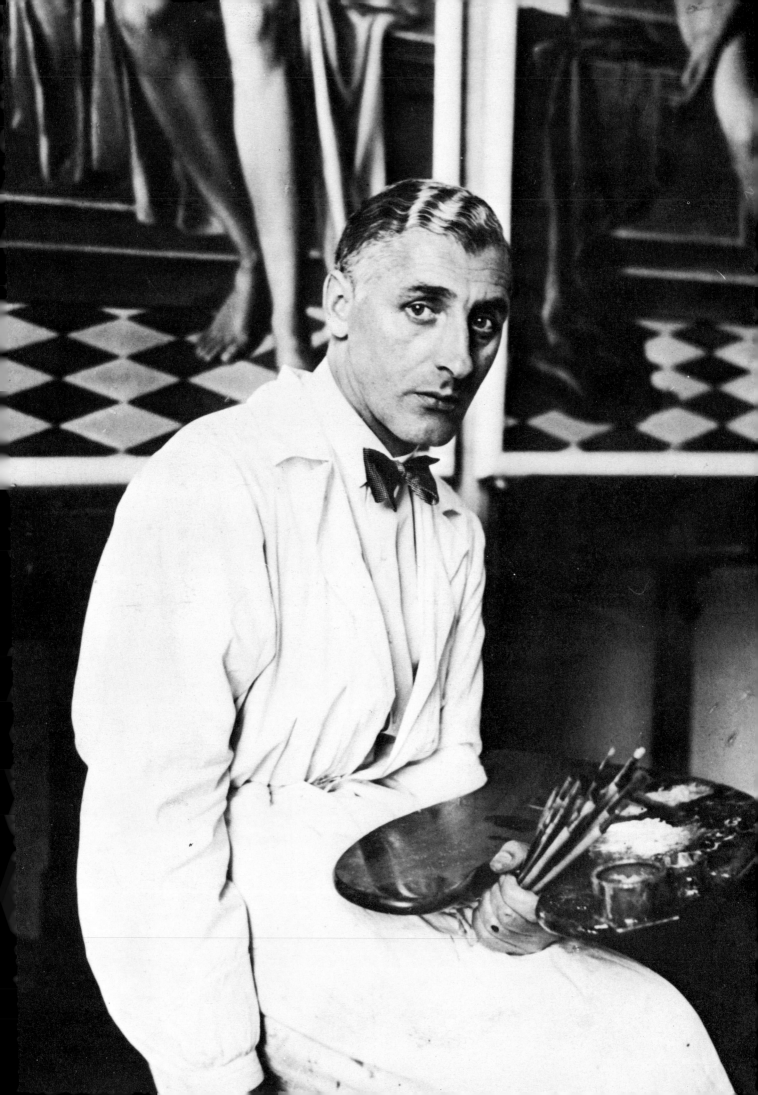

The Wilhelmstrasse on the
day of President von
Hindenburg's death,
2 August 1934. On that day
Hitler united the offices of
Chancellor and President
under the new title, Der
Führer.

Bad Wiessee not far from Munich, when they were un-ceremoniously dragged from their beds. Röhm was taken to a prison cell in Munich, where he was handed a pistol by two SS officers, who indicated that the best thing he could do would be to commit suicide. Röhm, understand-ably, demurred: 'If I am to be killed,' he said, 'let Adolf Hitler do it himself.' The two SS officers then did it for him.

As for Heines, he was discovered in bed with a young man—thus lending credence to charges that the SA was riddled with homosexuality and other perversions—and although accounts of his end differ, he was generally thought to have been taken to the road outside and there shot dead.

Also on 30 June General Kurt von Schleicher, who had recently begun to dabble again in politics, opened the front door of his villa outside Berlin to be confronted by a band of SS men in plain clothes, who shot both him and his newly-married wife dead on the spot.

There was one murder, however, that had nothing what-ever to do with politics, except by implication. On the same evening Dr Willi Schmidt, the music critic of a Munich newspaper, was playing his cello when some SS men burst into the room and took him away. Four days later his body was returned with strict instructions from the Gestapo to his widow that she was not to open the coffin 'in any circumstances.' Poor Dr Schmidt had been mistaken for

Above: Hitler and French Ambassador François-Ponçet (middle) admire a piece of French sculpture in 1937.
Above right: Professor Waetzoldt delivers a speech on the hundredth anniversary of the Berlin Museum.
Right: Model of the new Broadcast House in Berlin.
Far right: Hitler and Professor Troost's wife.
Below: Hitler proudly explains his plans for the reconstruction of Berlin, using a model.
Below right: The Museum of Art.
Below far right: Foyer of the Berlin Opera House in Charlottenburg after its redecoration by the Nazis.

The SA are issued new weapons. Banned from the streets by the Weimar Republic, the SA represented such a threat that it was purged and stripped of power by Hitler and the SS in the infamous Night of the Long Knives, 30 June 1934.

Left: Carl Stemmle with Erich Maria Remarque, whose *All Quiet on the Western Front* caused Nazis to protest vehemently against the showing of the film made of his book in 1929.

Below: The burning of the books on 11 May 1933 in the Opernplatz. Remarque's works were among them.

Far right: Ernst Röhm, who was killed in the Blood Purge with other Nazi leaders in 1934. Röhm was the leader of the SA which burned the 'un-German' literature.

another Willi Schmidt—a local SA leader—who had meanwhile also been shot.

Accounts of the numbers killed during the purge fluctuate wildly. Hitler admitted to 77 dead (which included three 'suicides'), but other sources quoted from 500 to a thousand. Certainly 150 SA leaders were rounded up in Berlin alone and executed by firing squads of Himmler's SS and Göring's special police at the cadet school at Lichterfelde.

That same summer President Hindenburg died, aged 87, and on his death it was announced that the offices of Chancellor and President were to be merged, and that Adolf Hitler would in consequence become both Head of State and Commander in Chief of the armed forces. All officers and men were obliged henceforth to swear the following oath of allegiance: 'I swear by God this sacred oath, that I will render unconditional obedience to Adolf Hitler, the Führer of the German Reich and people, Supreme Commander of the Armed Forces, and will be ready as a brave soldier to risk my life at any time for this oath.' For Hitler it was the ultimate triumph, but for the officer corps it was both an abrogation of responsibility and an admission of complicity—no longer could they turn away in disdain from the brutal excesses of the Nazi regime, for by association their hands were as blood-stained as any in the SS.

It was not only the Stormtroopers who suffered a purge. The cleansing force of Nazism permeated all aspects of German life. Racial purity was a *sine qua non*—but the tentacles of Nazi fanaticism spread to cover family life, the upbringing and education of children, Christianity and the arts. That most dangerous of Teutonic ideals, the myth of the 'German mode of being' which asserted the deep-down primordial sense of 'Germanness' once more reared its ugly head. And in the name of the primacy of German 'being,' human reason was denied its voice in the land, and in the name of Germanism countless crimes were committed against freedom of expression and the dignity of man.

One of the first crimes, a symbolic act of vandalism against truth and logic of barbaric simplicity, occurred on 10 May 1933. Students carrying lighted torches proceeded down the Unter den Linden to the University of Berlin, outside which they set fire to a huge pile of books—consisting of the work of such 'undesirable' German writers as Thomas and Heinrich Mann, Stefan Zweig, Erich Maria Remarque (whose novel *All Quiet on the Western Front* had shown just how unpleasant it could be to die for the Fatherland), Walther Rathenau, Albert Einstein, Alfred Kerr and Hugo Preuss (the professor who drafted the ill-fated Weimar constitution), together with many 'corrupt' foreign publications by writers such as Upton Sinclair, Helen Keller, H G Wells, Freud, André Gide, Emil Zola and Proust.

Their place on the nation's bookshelves was taken by large numbers of copies of Adolf Hitler's *Mein Kampf* (said

Above: Remarque and his wife at a tennis match in 1929 before the controversy was launched.

by Leon Feuchtwanger to contain '164,000 offenses against German grammar and syntax'), together with a few acceptable 'classics' such as Goethe and Schiller, and 'educational' novels such as the 'romantic peasant novel,' which extolled the virtues of motherhood, hard work, dedication to the Fatherland and selfless devotion to the Führer. Others in this genre were the anti-Jewish novel and the racial purity novel, in both of which the German people were seen to be uniquely endowed. But in the latter category it was not so much the Jews but the English, French or the Russians who were vilified, being variously described as 'biologically defective,' 'malevolent,' 'squinting,' or just plain 'debilitated.'

The responsibility for these purifying measures rested with Joseph Goebbels, appointed by Hitler Minister of Propaganda and Popular Enlightenment. In September 1933 a Reich Chamber of Culture had been created, with Göbbels as its President, which set itself the ambitious task of encouraging 'all forms of artistic creation or activity which are made public.' To achieve this end seven subordinate Chambers were established to direct and control literature, the fine arts, radio, the press, film, theater and music.

For Hitler the arts were 'the most important and effective part of culture.' Like the Kaiser, however, he was not in favor of any but the most representational painting, being strongly of the opinion that art should be uplifting rather than disturbing. Ugliness or painful reminders of the fallibility of human nature had no place in a Germany dedicated to raising the level of national consciousness to new heights. The public should only be allowed to see the beautiful and the picturesque—all the rest would have to go. In pursuit of this aesthetic ideal four appointed delegates, Professor Ziegler, Schweitzer-Mjölnir, Count Baudissin and Wolf Willrich, visited galleries and museums throughout the country in order to root out all 'degenerate' art. 'The swathe these four apocalyptic Norsemen cut through Germany's stored-up artistic treasure,' wrote Richard Gruneberger, 'has been estimated at upwards of 16,000 paintings, drawings, etchings and sculptures: 1000 pieces by Nolde, 700 by Haeckel, 600 each by Schmidt-Rottluff

Top left: Nazi sympathizers demonstrate against the showing of *All Quiet on the Western Front* in 1930.

Left: Berlin police protect the audience against Nazi demonstrators at the Nollendorfplatz where the film was shown.

The Platz der Republik
(earlier Königsplatz) in 1933.

Above: A German athlete brings the Olympic torch to the dais on the opening of the Berlin Olympics in 1936.

and Kirchner, 500 by Beckman, 400 by Kokoschka, 300 to 400 each by Hofer, Pechstein, Barlach, Feininger and Otto Müller, 200 to 300 each by Dix, Grosz and Corinth, 100 by Lehmbrück, as well as much smaller numbers of Cézannes, Picassos, Matisses, Gaugins, Van Goghs, Braques, Pisarros, Dufys, Chiricos and Max Ernsts.'

In 1937 a huge exhibition of 'degenerate' art was mounted in Munich—a public pillory of all the creative exploration of the past fifty years. The paintings were jumbled together without frames, 'as if arranged by fools or children' and many had offensive captions underneath ('Jewish desert-longings find expression,' 'German peasants looked at in the Yiddish manner'). Later in 1939 4000 canvases were burned in the courtyard of the Berlin Fire Brigade.

Eventually even artistic and literary criticism was banned —Goebbels justifying this move on the grounds that only the people themselves could be the judges of what they read and saw. 'Now,' he wrote, 'the public itself functions as critic, and through its participation or non-participation it pronounces clear judgment upon its poets, painters, composers and actors.'

Fed on a constant diet of pro-Nazi propaganda through the radio and the newspapers, it would have been surprising if they had been anything else. Goebbels, however, realized that total censorship of the press brought with it its own problems, but with the banning of all socialist and Communist publications after the Reichstag Fire, the

gradual takeover of newspapers and periodicals by the Nazis and the installation of 'government employed' editors, whose jobs depended on interpreting Nazi policy in wholly adulatory terms, formal censorship was virtually unnecessary. (In 1933 the Nazis owned 121 dailies and periodicals; by the end of 1934 they were directly responsible for 436 newspapers, and by 1944 they controlled 82 percent of the remaining 977.)

For propaganda purposes, however, the control of broadcasting was a coveted prize. At the opening of the radio exhibition in Berlin in August 1933, Joseph Goebbels quoted Napoleon, who had described the press as the 'seventh Great Power.' He continued: 'What the press was for the nineteenth century, wireless will be for the twentieth. One could alter the words of Napoleon, and call it the eighth Great Power.' Strangely, Hitler himself was an indifferent broadcaster. He needed physical contact with the masses, the 'acoustic backcloth' of applause, chants of 'Sieg Heil,' and lighting effects to obtain maximum rapport with his audience.

Film was far more effective. Goebbels considered it the most powerful medium of all (and not entirely because of his personal interest in film actresses). Leni Riefenstahl, whose documentary film *Triumph des Willens*, (1935) was a masterpiece of emotive spectacle, took as her subject the party congress at Nuremberg of 4-10 September 1934. William Shirer attended that same congress and, although by no means a convert to Nazism, which he resisted tooth and claw, was nevertheless swept away by the pageantry. 'I'm beginning to comprehend,' he wrote in his diary, '. . . some of the reasons for Hitler's astounding success . . . he is restoring pageantry and color and mysticism to the drab lives of twentieth-century Germans. This morning's opening meeting in the Luitpold Hall on the outskirts of Nuremberg was more than a gorgeous show; it also had something of the mysticism and religious fervor of an Easter or Christmas Mass in a great Gothic Cathedral.' Bands played, lights flickered over the stage, an 'immense symphony orchestra' played Beethoven's *Egmont* Overture. Small wonder that, aided and abetted by the gifted direction of Leni Riefenstahl and a stirring musical score by

Below: Leni Riefenstahl and Heinrich Himmler of the SS (left) during the filming of *Triumph of the Will* in 1934 at the Nuremburg rallies.

Herbert Windt, it became one of the most powerful documentaries ever made.'

With the virtual nationalization of the film industry in 1937 the cinema went the way of all the other Nazi-dominated subordinate chambers and became a slave to party doctrine. In 1936 the Olympic Games were held in Berlin and two years later Leni Riefenstahl's film of the event, *Olympia*, was given a gala performance on the occasion of Hitler's forty-ninth birthday. It was her undisputed masterpiece and a stunning testament to the ambivalent power of film—it has still not been decided whether it was a blatant piece of propaganda or merely a brilliant record of athletic skill made by an admirer of the Nazi regime. One left-wing critic wrote: 'Leni Riefenstahl's films about the Olympic Games . . . are, even in their purified versions that evade mention of Hitler and other Nazi leaders, still outspokenly fascistic in spirit . . .' however another, less subjective commentator felt that, 'Neither *Triumph des Willens* nor *Olympia* could have been made by a

Below: Berlin's Olympic Stadium, built west of Charlottenburg, during the Games in August 1936.

Field Marshal von Mackensen, Hitler, Interior Minister
Frick and SS-Führer Julius Schaub enjoy the Olympic
Games in Berlin.

Above: Leni Riefenstahl during the filming of *Olympia* which was released in 1938.

propagandist pure and simple. They are evidently the work of an artist, even if an artist of an immensely naive political nature. . . .'

Not all films of the Third Reich were of the high quality of *Triumph des Willens*, and *Olympia*. Many were simply anti-Semitic. By far the most notorious of this genre was *Jud Süss*. As one film historian wrote, 'It brought disgrace and worse on almost everyone connected with it, and was in the public limelight when it became the central exhibit in . . . postwar trial for crimes against humanity.' Blatantly provocative and crudely violent it had an apparently instantly inflammatory effect on adolescents—although supposedly banned for viewers under fourteen, many cinema proprietors turned a blind eye in the cause of indoctrination. Many cases were recorded of Jews being attacked by bands of youths who had just sat through the film.

Anti-Semitism, however, was a disease from which the Third Reich was unwilling and unable to be cured. Although Max Reinhardt had gone, together with other Jewish directors, producers and actors, the theater was less tainted than the other media. The classics were, after all, the classics, and nothing much could be done to turn them into instruments of propaganda. And, as William Shirer pointed out, the Nazi playwrights were on the whole so 'ludicrously bad' that even the brain-washed Berlin theater-going public stayed away.

As for music, 'From the seizure of power onwards,' wrote Richard Gruneberger 'the regime bathed the country in music as in a foetal fluid.' (At the Nuremberg rallies Wagner's *Die Meistersinger* floated above the tramping feet, Liszt's Preludes were relayed over the radio before the 'victory communiques,' and Hitler's suicide was announced to the strains of Bruckner's *Seventh Symphony*.) Many composers, conductors and performers had left the country either in disgust or because they were Jewish, but some stayed. Richard Strauss became the first President of the Reich Chamber of Music, and Wilhelm Furtwängler remained to conduct the Philharmonic. Inevitably, of course, there were 'degenerate' composers whose work was forbidden. Severus Ziegler, (manager of the Weimar Theater and brother of the Professor so active in removing unsuitable pictures from German galleries) mounted a 'degenerate music' exhibition, where, predictably, Mahler, Schönberg, Stravinsky, Hindemith and Weill were all held up to public ridicule.

The opera flourished, although many seemingly innocent works had to be expunged from the repertoire. Even Mozart was not immune—the libretti for *The Marriage of Figaro* and *Cosi Fan Tutti* having been written by a baptized Jew, Lorenzo da Ponte, and *The Magic Flute* having treasonably masonic overtones. The Berlin Opera, des-

Right: The poet's balcony on the Gertraudten Bridge.
Far right: Berlin's oldest weapons-smith in the Molkenstrasse. Old Berlin was devastated a few years after these pictures were taken in 1937.

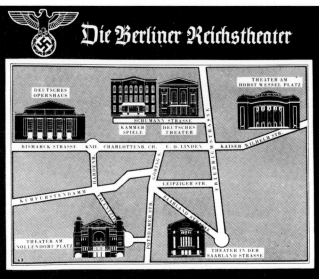

perate for an enlargement of their ever-shrinking program, was obliged to resurrect hitherto little-known works such as Weber's *Euryanthe* and Humperdinck's *Königskinder*.

The musical education of children in schools, however, was said to have fallen away sharply during the Third Reich—as one professor of music commented: 'Private musical instruction has declined to an alarming extent. . . . Children are so much in demand by their organizations that they have no more time for practising. . . .' 'Organization,' in this case, was a euphemism for 'Hitler Youth,' for after 1933 all other youth clubs were closed down. Formed in 1922 and overtly political in character, it retained, until after the Nazis came to power, a clandestine and illegal nature which rendered it doubly attractive to the fanatically-inclined adolescent. After 1933 it came out into the open and became a breeding ground for the SS. Gone were the innocent days of the 'Wandervögel' (founded in 1901 in the Berlin suburb of Streglitz by a young shorthand writer called Hermann Hoffmann) whose followers sought merely to escape from parental and educational restrictions into the countryside, there to ramble, picnic and sing forgotten folk songs to the accompaniment of a lute or a guitar. The Wandervögel hungered for romance, adventure and for purity of ideals. The Hitler Youth, as one member wrote severely, 'is aware not only of the great influence of education, but especially of the practical experience of life. If German youth today takes hikes, it does not do so with a false and gushing sentimentality intoxicated with Nature, but . . . subordinates its action to a political purpose. German youth roams the countryside in order to know its fatherland, and, above all, comrades in other parts of the Reich.'

In their Führer Adolf Hitler, the Youth Movement had a God ideally tailored to its needs. Although not given to exercise, (he did not play games and never rode or swam), he had admirably 'simple' tastes—he did not smoke or drink, was apparently 'indifferent to the clothes he wore' and took women in moderation, and rarely very seriously. His plans for the Fatherland exactly coincided with the latent desires of Germany's burgeoning youth—the promises of glory, the purity of the German race, the sense of corporate national will, all so sadly lacking in the corrupt days of the Weimar Republic.

Like many autocrats Hitler needed imposing surroundings. He felt that Berlin (which at one time he thought of renaming 'Germania') was not grand enough. He looked back enviously to the days of Frederick the Great when Berlin had been transformed according to the whim of one man. Like Frederick (for whom he nourished a profound admiration) he admired the classical style and he determined to do likewise.

In 1936 he summoned the architect Albert Speer and outlined the plans he had for the capital. He wanted a wide avenue on the northern side of which would be a huge

Left: View from the tower of the Kaiser Wilhelm Memorial Church on the Tauentzienstrasse in 1937.
Top: The Unter den Linden at night in 1937 lit up with Nazi eagles.
Above: The Friedrichstrasse at the corner of the Behrenstrasse in 1937.

Below: The Alexanderplatz in the summer of 1939.
Bottom: The Dom and the River Spree in the twilight of Berlin in 1939.
Right: The famous Café Kranzler on the Kurfürstendamm in 1939, one of the few survivors of the war.

meeting hall, 'a domed structure into which St Peter's Cathedral in Rome would have fitted several times over.' To balance this gigantic building, Hitler suggested an 'arc of triumph 400 feet high.' It would, he said 'be a worthy monument to our dead of the First World War.'

Night after night Speer visited Hitler in his rooms in the new Chancellery in the Voss Strasse, and night after night they pored over plans for vast palaces and ministries, two enormous railway stations and a lake 3300 feet long and 1155 feet wide.'

Despite his dreams for the city, Hitler never liked Berlin. He felt more at home in the Berghof, his Bavarian house at Obersalzburg, to which he retreated at more and more frequent intervals, summoning his reluctant Ministers to confer with him there. After the outbreak of the Second World War plans for the development of Berlin were put in abeyance, although Hitler still planned to have it rebuilt for his victory parade in 1950. On the occasion of his visit to Paris following the fall of France in 1940, he was moved to say to Speer: 'Wasn't Paris beautiful? But Berlin must be made more beautiful. In the past I often considered whether or not we would have to destroy Paris. But when we are finished in Berlin, Paris will be only a shadow. So why should we destroy it?' Even Speer was shocked by this potential act of vandalism.

It was not Paris but his own capital city which was to be destroyed, and Hitler himself would die beneath it, his dreams unfulfilled. On 18 July 1940, however, with Germany in an optimistic trance of delight over her victories in

the west, a huge parade was held in Berlin. William Shirer was there: 'For the first time,' he wrote in his diary, 'since 1871 German troops staged a victory parade through the Brandenburg Gate. . . . Nothing pleases the Berliners—a naive and simple people on the whole—more than a good military parade. And nothing more than an afternoon off from their dull jobs and their dismal homes. I mingled among the crowds in the Pariserplatz. A holiday spirit ruled completely. Nothing martial about the mass of the people here. . . . Looking at them, I wondered if any of them understood what was going on in Europe, if they had an inkling that their joy, that this victorious parade of the goose-steppers, was based on a great tragedy for millions of others whom these troops and the leaders of these people had enslaved.'

If the reality of war was remote from Berliners in July it was no longer so by August. Despite all assurances to the contrary the British started to bomb the city. On 25 August the first bombs fell—'it was,' Shirer admitted, 'a magnificent, a terrible sight. . . .' He continued: 'The Berliners are stunned. They did not think it could happen: When this war began Göring assured them it couldn't. . . . And then last night the guns all over the city suddenly began pounding and you could hear the British motors humming directly overhead, and from all reports there was a pell-mell, frightened rush to the cellars by the five million people who live in this town.'

The horrors of the bombing had only just begun. After the Casablanca conference of 1943 the 'combined bomber offensive' was launched—the USAAF bombing during the daytime and the RAF during the night. As a result of this concerted attack, one and a half million Berliners were

Below: Nazi car warns Berliners not to buy 'Jewish goods' in front of a Jewish-owned shop.

Above: Jewish-owned shop is placarded by Nazis. Within two years of the Nazi takeover few businesses were still controlled by German Jews. Hitler legitimized the seizure of Jewish property by passing the Nuremburg Laws in 1935.

left homeless, between thirty and 55,000 killed and about 75,000 wounded. Thirty thousand houses were completely destroyed and 167,927 left 'partly habitable.' Ursula von Kardoff, a journalist wrote in her diary on 3 February 1945 after the worst raids of the war, 'Why doesn't anyone go crazy? Why doesn't anybody go into the streets and shout, "I've had enough." Why isn't there a revolution? . . .'

On 20 July 1944 there nearly was a revolution. Colonel Claus Schenk von Stauffenberg, reporting to Hitler's headquarters in East Prussia, took with him a briefcase which contained a bomb. He placed it under the wooden table round which Hitler and 24 others were seated, and then left the room, giving the excuse that he had to telephone Berlin. Hitler survived the attack—the bomb killed those nearest to it, but merely singed the Führer's hair, damaged one arm and blew off one of his trouser legs. His revenge was terrible. Count von Stauffenberg and four other conspirators were shot in a small courtyard at the back of the Bendlerblock, and eight others were hanged in particularly gruesome circumstances. Nearly 10,000 more within the officer corps suspected of 'apathy towards the regime' were either executed or sent to concentration camps.

Count von Stauffenberg attempted to speed up what the

Allies were inexorably achieving. The end of the 'Thousand-year Reich' came in Wagnerian splendor, the flames consuming the buildings of Berlin 'roaring with blast-furnace heat.' And deep in his bunker under the city Hitler waited, raging against the inefficiencies of his generals, while above his head the people of Berlin prepared to defend themselves against the onslaught of the Russians.

By 26 April 1945 Berlin was surrounded. *Der Panzerbar*, a four-page news sheet, the last Nazi newspaper to be printed in Berlin, had as its headline: 'Bulwark against Bolshevism! Berlin: A Mass-Grave for Soviet Tanks! Berlin fights for the Reich and for Europe!' Four days later Hitler shot himself through the mouth, seated in front of a portrait of Frederick the Great. On 1 May Joseph Goebbels and his wife ordered an SS man to shoot them.

The following day the city surrendered, and, as Walter Henry Nelson wrote, 'When the last gun was put away, Berlin looked like the landscape of the moon, its streets a mere succession of craters, and along the edges of its boulevards a few trembling walls, where houses had once stood. The air was sickly sweet from thousands of corpses lying about in the streets, in the denuded parks and under the ruins. Here and there, a few houses still stood, pockmarked with bullet holes, their windowpanes scattered about the streets. Their walls bore either Hitler's last call to ultimate resistance or the very first message posted by the Soviets: 'Hitlers come and go, but the German people and the German state go on.' It was an apt epitaph.

JSRAEL
N. JSRA
Deutsche!
Wehrt Euch!
Kauft nicht bei Juden!
Deutsche!
Wehrt Euch!
Kauft nicht bei Juden!

The signs read: "Deutsche! Wehrt Euch! Kauft nicht bei Juden!"

Top: Hundreds wait to congratulate the Führer on his 46th birthday on 20 April 1935.
Above: The Jewish boycott at Israel's department store in 1933. By 1935 it was in Nazi hands.

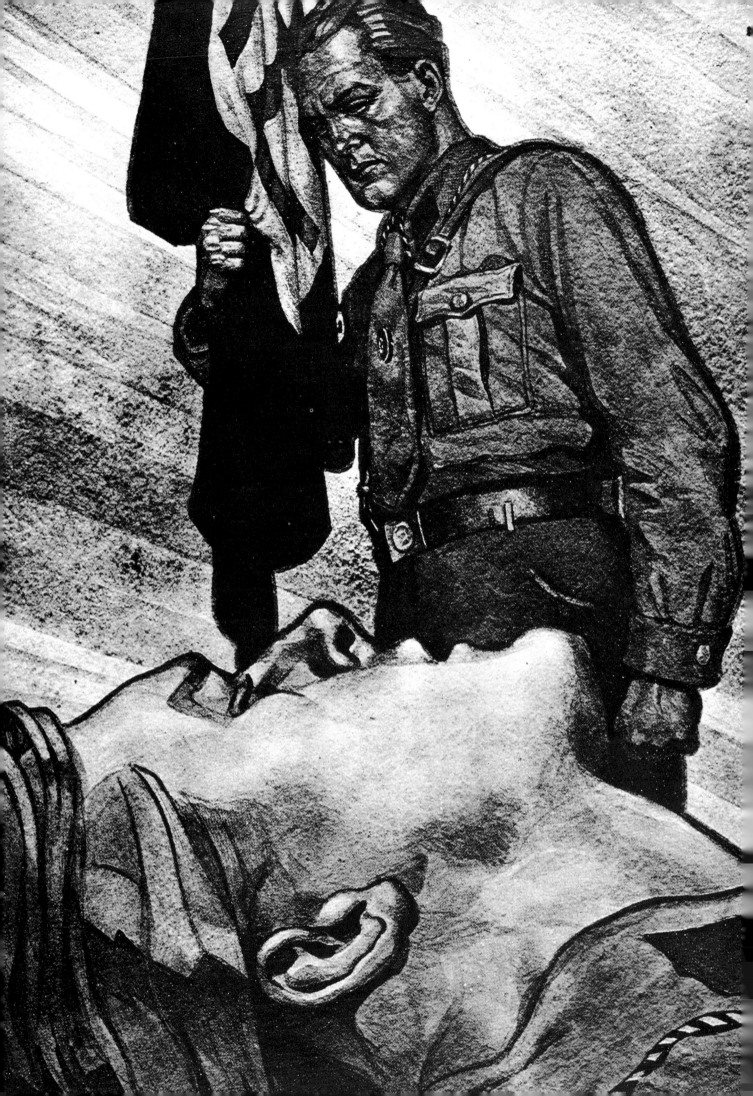

Two posters commemorating the SA-men who fell in the street-fighting for Nazism before 1933.

Previous spread left: A Nazi poster.
Previous spread right: A Communist anti-Hitler cartoon.
Left: Communist poster tots up the cost of an SA uniform.
Above: Social Democratic poster.
Right: Berlin postwoman in Nazi uniform in 1940.
Below: In the Beginning was the Word.

NAZI PROPAGANDA

Berlin streets, as in all other cities of Germany, were overwhelmed by a rush of Nazi propaganda posters which were produced with a regularity only matched by their macabre, artistic excellence. The face of Berlin was changing rapidly as the Nazi Party took over every element of German national life. The posters here are a few examples of the propaganda machine in action.

Left: Mother and Child. The Nazis promoted family life in the service of the State.

Below left: People to people and blood to blood; your Yes for the Führer.

Below: The Eternal Jew, a poster for a virulently anti-Semitic film.

Right: Blood and Soil was the slogan used for a farmers' rally in Goslar in 1937 and was repeated in other contexts before the war.

Left: Students from all over the country came to Munich for a rally supporting the tenth anniversary of the National Socialist Student League in 1936.

Above: 'If you save five marks a week, then you will be able to drive your own car' was the slogan of this early Volkswagen advertisement. Millions joined this hire purchase scheme but few drove the KdF-wagen (strength through joy car), as it was called. The money was confiscated in 1939 for the war effort.

Above right: This poster supported large, happy German families. As in some other European countries, families were given special tax allowances and outright stipends to reproduce as quickly as possible.

Right: This poster urged all Germans to vote for a Greater Germany in 1938 after the incorporation of Austria into the Reich. Few negative votes were cast.

Overleaf left: Poster celebrating Reichs Party Day for Peace in 1939. The rally was successful though the sentiments were not.

Overleaf right: A 1932 election poster for the Nazis who promised work, freedom and bread.

Reichsparteitag des Friedens
1939

LOST E

Below: The ruins of the Reichstag after Berlin fell to the
Russian armies, 7 May 1945.
Bottom: Berlin today. The center of Berlin shifted to the
west as East Berlin was incorporated into the German
Democratic Republic.

EAST

GERMANY

West

Tegel
Airport

East

Berlin

River Spree

KURFÜRSTENDAMM

Berlin

Tempelhof
Airport

| 0 | MILES | 8 |
| 0 | KILOMETERS | 12 |

ERLIN

INDEX

Numbers in italics refer to pages on which references to illustrations occur

Acknowledgments

The author and publisher would like to thank the follqwing people who have helped in the preparation of this book: David Eldred, who designed it; Catherine Bradley, who edited it; Richard Natkiel, who drew the maps; Rolf Steinberg, who did the picture research; Susan Piquemal, who prepared the index.

Picture Credits

The pictures were supplied by the Bundesarchiv, Coblenz except for the following:

Ullstein: 41, 44–45 (bottom), 55 (top left), 57, 66–67, 68–69, 74 (top right), 75 (top), 76–77 (bottom 3), 78, 79 (center and bottom), 82 (top), 83, 84–85, 86, 90, 91 (top), 92 (top), 92–93, 93 (top 3), 100–101, 102 (bottom), 103 (top), 104–105, 161, 162–163, 164 (top), 168 (top), 170, 171.
Landesbildstelle Berlin: 8–9, 11, 12 (top), 14, 15 (bottom), 19 (bottom), 21 (bottom), 22 (top), 72 (top), 82 (bottom 2), 87, 94, 95 (bottom), 102 (top), 106, 110 (left), 111, 112, 113, 114–115, 118 (bottom right), 126–127, 136–137, 172–173, 183 (bottom).
Rolf Steinberg: 8 (inset), 9 (top), 10, 25 (top), 47, 58–59, 62–63, 64–65, 91 (bottom),

142, 143 (top), 151, 153, 154–155, 156, 157, 174 (top), 175, 179, 180–181.
Bison Picture Library: 27, 34–35, 44–45 (top), 53, 60–61, 98 (top), 99 (bottom), 110 (right), 117, 120 (both), 132 (right), 139 (top 2), 150, 152, 165 (bottom 2 and center right), 169 (top), 176–177, 190–191, 192, 196 (top), 197, 198, 199, 200, 201.
Bildarchiv Preussischer Kulturbesitz: 43, 76 (top), 80–81 (bottom), 107 (bottom), 116, 117–118, 118 (bottom left), 132 (top), 132 (bottom left).
Suhrkamp Verlag: 93 (below).
Novosti: 202–203.
Staatsbibliothek: 74–75.